HISTORY

OF THE

EUCHARIST

Roger Skrenes

En Route Books and Media, LLC

Saint Louis, MO

⊕*ENROUTE*
Make the time

En Route Books and Media, LLC
5705 Rhodes Avenue
St. Louis, MO 63109

Cover credit: TJ Burdick
Cover image: Juan de Juanes, "The Last Supper"
(circa 1560)

Revised Edition ISBN-13: 978-0-99911-435-3
Library of Congress Control Number: 2017956377

First Edition Published 2017
Revised Edition Published 2024

DEDICATION

To Sister Celesta
my eighth grade teacher
who could not get the chalk
off her fingers.

To my parents
who took me to Mass.

To faithful theologians
who help us see
the deeper mysteries
of our faith.

To Father George Macrae, SJ
my generous instructor
in the Gospel of John.

Table of Contents

Foreword

In my book *Liturgy 101: Sacraments & Sacramentals* (Liguori Publications, 2010), I devote a chapter to the Most Holy Eucharist. Here, Roger Skrenes devotes a whole book to it, and, indeed, one could devote a whole library.

I note in my book that Christians have endowed the Eucharist with more titles than any other sacrament.

The word "Eucharist" itself comes from the Greek word meaning "to give thanks," and reflects the fact that our Lord "gave thanks" at the Last Supper (Mark 14:23).

The Second Vatican Council called this sacrament the "divine sacrifice of the Eucharist" (SC 2), the "sacrifice of the Mass" (SC 7, 12, 49), and "the mystery of faith" (SC 48).

Pope Leo XIII emphasized that the "bread of life" (John 6:48) is God's gift, the chief of all gifts that God extends to humanity, and the gift "than which nothing can be more excellent or more conductive to salvation" (MC 5).

Saint Thomas Aquinas aptly described the Eucharist as the "perfection of every perfection," and liturgical books refer to the "Most Holy Eucharist."

All the sacraments are perfect and holy, but the Church calls the Eucharist the "Most Holy Sacrament" or the "Sacrament of sacraments" (CCC 1330) because of Christ's unique Presence in it.

Roger Skrenes' book provides a solid explanation as to why.

Dr Daniel Van Slyke, J.D., Ph.D.

Introduction

The Eucharist is not a topic of the moment. Like any good teacher, God took "his time" in revealing the Eucharist. This is in keeping with the facts that "God is love" [1 John 4:8] and that true love is "patient and is kind" [1 Corinthians 13:4].

> "The Lord is slow about his promise … is patient with you, not wanting any to perish …" [2 Peter 3:9].

The Eucharist has been revealed slowly, step by step, throughout Biblical history. In this history there are two main tracks.

First, there is the history of bread and its use in the OT. In Abraham's time, Melchizedek brought out bread and wine for celebration [Genesis 14:18]. In Moses' time, God gave the Hebrew people the miraculous bread-like "Manna" on the desert floor for forty years [Exodus 16:35]. Bread and wine were also used for sacrifice during the whole of Israel's history. Finally, all these elements came together at the Last

Supper, when Christ gave himself to the world by way of the consecrated Bread of the Eucharist.

Second, there is the sacrificial lamb of the OT Passover. At that time, God ordered the Hebrew people to offer a lamb on the eve of their "exodus" from Egypt. God then proceeded to "pass over" the Hebrews with his final plague on Egyptian soil - as the Hebrews honored his Presence.

After the Exodus from Egypt, Israel would sacrifice a lamb each morning and evening to thank God for this overarching care of his people. This practice continued throughout Israel's history. The story of the lamb within Israel's past would eventually become a symbol, or foreshadowing, of the life of Christ. A biographical picture was revealed during the time of Isaiah with the account of the "suffering servant" of the Lord [Isaiah 53:1-12]. In this account, the Servant dies as a sacrificial lamb for the world's sin. However, at the time and as time went by, no one knew who the lamb of Isaiah 53 was. Then, finally, in the NT era it was revealed that Jesus of Nazareth, the Christ, was the "Lamb of God." John the Baptist announced it.

> "John [the Baptist] saw Jesus coming toward him and said: 'Behold the Lamb of God who takes away the sin of the world.'" John 1:29

Finally, at the Last Supper, itself a Passover meal, Jesus revealed himself as the historic Lamb of Isaiah 53:1-12. Then, he offered himself in the Eucharist as the new "Passover Lamb" of the new era [1 Corinthians 5:7-8].

The focal point of these two separate tracks was the Last Supper, and then finally "the cross." However, the story of the Lamb did not end there. The real ending of this whole story was the Resurrection of Christ and his ongoing Presence for us in Heaven.

This book will examine these elements of the Eucharist and others as well.

Book Cover Design for Memorize the Mass!
(En Route Books and Media, 2016), authored by Kevin Vost

1.

God's Presence in Creation

The Holy Spirit has revealed to the Biblical prophets that "God is love" [1 John 4:8]. Love by its very nature is reciprocal; someone is present to share the love of the person loving. Within the Godhead, the eternal lovers are God the Father, his Word, the Son, and the Holy Spirit. Three Persons of one divine Nature. Many times within the New Testament [NT], Jesus would speak of this love relationship within the Trinity.

> "All was given Me [Jesus] by my Father, and no one knows the Son except the Father, and no one knows the Father except the Son." Matthew 11:27

> "I [Jesus] and my Father are one." John 10:30

> "Father … you loved me before the foundation of the world." John 11:24

"Believe me that I [Jesus] am in the Father and the Father is in me; or else believe the works [the miracles I do that prove this]." John 14:11

"I will pray to the Father and he will give you … the Spirit of truth … and he [the Spirit] will teach you all things, and bring all things to your remembrance, whatsoever I [Jesus] have said to you." John 14:16-17 & 26

"The Spirit of truth, who proceeds from the Father, shall testify of me [Jesus]." John 15:26

"Father, glorify me [again] … with the glory I had with you before the world was … I have given them [on earth] the words which you [Father] gave me [to say while here]." John 17:5-8

This "overflowing" love within the Godhead throws light upon the question as to why God would choose to create a world where intelligent creatures could share his own joy. Such a world would be developed from "matter," which God called into existence from nothing. From this initial start out of nothing, God would slowly evolve the world into what we see around us today. He would use secondary causes in this effort. The way this worked out looks something like this:

1.	Big Bang [the start]	13.7 billion years ago
2.	Stars	13.3 billion
3.	Our Sun & Earth	4.5 billion
4.	Plants on earth	3 billion
5.	One-celled animals	1 billion
6.	Fish	500 million
7.	Amphibians	400 million
8.	Reptiles [scales]	300 million
9.	Mammals [hair]	200 million
10.	Small Primates [lemurs]	50 million
11.	Apes	10 million
12.	People	2 million

It has further been revealed to the prophets of the Bible that through this long process God has created human beings in his own image: having both intelligence and will power.

"In the image of God he created them." Genesis 1:26

This meant that, like God, human beings would have an <u>intellect</u> to know the world around them, a <u>will</u> to act within the world and upon it, and an accommodating <u>memory</u> to hold one's life together while providing it with identity. The <u>intellect</u> of a person would correspond to God the Father; the <u>will</u> to God the Son acting within the world [John 1:1-3 & 14]; and <u>memory</u> as the Holy Spirit, who "knows the deep things of God" [1 Corinthians 2:10].

And so in creation God began to reveal himself to people on this planet, his Presence being built into the very fabric of a person's life, thereby explaining why human beings are drawn to the divine mind.

The Sistine Chapel, Michelangelo (1508-1512)
Courtesy of Wikipedia

2.

Sacrifice: Trying to Reach God

God created human beings as an image of himself [Genesis 1:26]. Made in this way people have generally been drawn toward the divine. However, God has not generally disclosed himself visibly to humans. Not until the coming of Christ would most humans experience God in a visible form on this earth.

> "No man has ever seen God [the Father]; the only begotten Son [Jesus], in the presence of the Father, has declared him." John 1:18

Each person who has come into the world has had an inborn pull toward the divine. Unconsciously, humans see this divine Presence in many places. Even though people could not see God visibly, they nevertheless associated mysterious aspects of life on earth and in the heavens with the divine. Some thought that the sun was an actual divine Presence because it provided warmth and causes plants to grow in its light. So early humans worshipped the sun. Others saw a human face on the moon's surface and imagined it to be a divine person. In another example, the experience of being "in love" revealed an abundant kind of life within the lovers, so love was viewed as part of the divine. Thus there has been in every culture a "goddess of love." Also, the vastness and unceasing activity of the ocean was seen as a god. It was also observed that plants and animals cannot live very long without water. Water brings life. And so the ocean was worshipped. Lightning storms were also observed, speaking thunderously from on high. And so thunderstorms were viewed as a cover for some mysterious god or gods.

People therefore went on to worship various speculative notions of the divine. They expressed this worship in various ways. One way, of special importance, was the ritual practice of "sacrifice." In sacrifice, something of value was "offered up," or surrendered to the god or goddess. This surrendering may have been small, such as a plant item, or it may have been large, such as a goat or a cow. By giving up this valuable item the person deprived himself of its possession or use. It was also a sign of one's dependence upon the god or goddess and a way of seeking his or her protection in life.

Sacrifice to the gods was done in many places on this planet. There were essentially three kinds of "sacrifice." First, there was total sacrifice or "holocaust." "Holo" means "whole"; "caust" means "burnt." This involved the burning of the whole animal on an altar. The animal was usually a cow, sheep, or goat. The animal's blood, thought to be the source of its life, was removed from its body and sprinkled on the sides of the altar. This was a way of returning the animal's life to the deity. The animal's body was then completely burned. The odor from the burning flesh was thought to rise up to the deity as a form of worship or prayer.

Later, in Israel's history, various kinds of burnt offerings came to represent the whole people. There was, for example, a daily offering in the Temple of Jerusalem of one lamb in the morning and another lamb in the evening [Exodus 29:38-39 & Numbers 28:4]. During Passover, each year, several animals were offered at the Temple [Numbers 28:19]. This was also true on the Day of Atonement [Numbers 29:8] and on the Feast of Tabernacles [Numbers 29:13].

Another kind of sacrifice was that of the "thanksgiving offering." In Hebrew, the word used to speak of this offering was "todah." It was offered by individuals who believed they had received a blessing of some kind: who might have been, for example, saved from death [Psalm 56:12-13] or had overcome some kind of trouble [Psalm 116:16-17].

> "He shall offer ... the sacrifice of thanksgiving ..." Leviticus 7:13

> "Let them sacrifice the sacrifices of thanksgiving, and declare God's works with rejoicing." Psalm 107:22

> "I will take the cup of salvation and ... I will offer the sacrifice of thanksgiving and call upon the name of Yahweh." Psalm 116:13 and 17

> "Offer a sacrifice of thanksgiving with leaven ... children of Israel." Amos 4:5

The thanksgiving sacrifice could also involve a meal. Part of the sacrificed animal was assigned to the priest who made the offering. The other part of the meat went to the person or persons who brought the offering. This person who "made the sacrifice" ate a meal before God with his family. The meal often included "unleavened cakes" [Leviticus 7:12-13]. This kind of meal was viewed as a form of "communion" with the deity, just as meals among humans today often seal or deepen relationships.

> "Jacob offered sacrifice ... and called his brothers to eat bread." Genesis 31:54

> "You shall eat before Yahweh your God, and shall rejoice in all [the ways] God has blessed you." Deuteronomy 12:7

Jesus would later use this kind of sacrifice at the Last Supper. Jesus shared a meal with his apostles, then took bread, "gave thanks" [Eucharist means 'thanksgiving'], saying that in the future such consecrated Bread would be "my Body ... given for you." Thus, Jesus introduced into the world his continuing Presence.

A third kind of sacrifice used by ancient peoples was that of the "sin offering." Everyone sins!

> "God did not make death, nor does He rejoice in the destruction of the living … God formed man to be imperishable [to go directly to Heaven]; in the image of his own nature He made them." Wisdom 1:13 and 2:23

> "By one man [Adam] sin entered the world, and death by sin, and so [death] passed on to all men for all men [down to the present time] have sinned." Romans 5:12

> "I [King David] was brought forth in iniquity and in sin did my mother conceive me." Psalm 51:5

> "The imagination of man's heart is evil from his youth." Genesis 8:21

> "We have sinned with our fathers." Psalm 106:6

"No one living is just in your sight [God]."
Psalm 143:2

"Our fathers have sinned … we [the off-spring] have borne their sins." Lamentations 5:7

"There is not a righteous man on earth who does [only] good and does not sin." Ecclesiastes 7:20

"If we say that we have no sin, we deceive ourselves, and the truth is not in us." 1 John 1:8

Almost everyone feels obliged to do something about personal sin. The "sin offering" was one way for early peoples to place sin in the deity's hands and ask forgiveness. It was a way of trying to purify oneself. Expiation sacrifices were offered to reestablish "communion" with the deity that had been interrupted by sin. It was thought, for example, that when the person offering placed his hands upon the animal, he was unloading personal sins upon the victim. These sins would then be removed as the victim was sacrificed.

They would "go up" in the smoke to God for forgiveness.

Later, in Israel, sin offerings were commonly used.

> "Aaron and his sons shall eat the flesh of the
> ram [male sheep] and the bread that is in the
> basket … They shall eat those things [of the
> sin offering] by which forgiveness is made …
> to sanctify themselves …for they [the offer-
> ings] are holy." Exodus 29:32-34

The coming of Christ marked the end of animal and plant sacrifices as a valid form of worship. The book of Hebrews questioned whether such offerings could truly perfect the inner self of a person.

> "It is not possible that the blood of bulls and
> goats should take away sins." Hebrews 10:4

In the NT, Jesus replaced animal sacrifice with the offering of himself for our sin. He became mankind's offering for sin when he died upon the cross. Though he himself was without sin, he took sin upon himself, as an offering for everyone.

"Now once at the end of the world he [Christ] has appeared to put away sin by the sacrifice of himself ... Christ was offered once to bear the sins of many." Hebrews 9:26-28

"God [the Father] was in Christ reconciling the world to himself ... The one [Christ], who had not known sin, was made to be sin on behalf of us, that we might become in him [in Christ] the righteousness of God [the Father]." 2 Corinthians 5:19-21

On the day when Jesus rose from the dead, he gave his Church this power to raise people from the dead of their sin. On Easter Sunday, he appeared to his apostles and said the following words:

"Peace be to you. As [God] the Father has sent me [Jesus], even so I send you ... Receive the Holy Spirit. Whoever's sins you forgive, they are forgiven them." John 20:21-22

This is the Sacrament of Reconciliation [or Confession]. Earlier in his ministry Jesus said a similar thing to his Apostles [and their successor bishops]:

"Whatsoever you loose on earth [in the future] shall be loosed in Heaven." Matthew 18:18

3.

Abraham & the Impossible

God appeared to Abraham for the first time when he was 75 years old. Abraham lived in Haran about 600 miles north of Canaan [what would eventually be called "Israel"]. Abraham was told by God to move to Canaan where God would make him a "great nation" so that "in you all the families of earth shall be blessed" [Genesis 12:1-4].

Abraham did as God commanded, but 24 years later, God had still not given him a son through his wife, Sarah. How would God's promises to Abraham be fulfilled? Then, God appeared to Abraham when he was 99 years old to establish a covenant with him and announce that his son, Isaac, would be born.

"When Abraham was 99 years old, the lord appeared to him and said ... I will establish my covenant between me and you and your seed [offspring] after you ... for an ever-lasting covenant, to be a God to you and to your seed after you. And I will give to you … all the land of Canaan [modern Israel] for an everlasting possession; and I will be their God." Genesis 17:1 and 7

In other words, God is going to reveal himself to the Hebrew people and be their God forever! This promise to be their God is at the heart of God's agreement with Israel.

"I will give them a heart to know Me … and I will be their God." Jeremiah 24:7

"I will put my Law … in their hearts and will be their God." Jeremiah 31:33

"House of Israel … I am your God." Ezekiel 34:30-31

"I will say to them … 'You are my people'; and they shall say, 'You [Yahweh] are my God.'" Hosea 2:23

"Jerusalem … they shall be my people and I shall be their God." Zechariah 8:8

However, how could God keep his promises without a firstborn son to begin Abraham's genealogy? At this point, God announces that Isaac will be born in Abraham's 100th year!

> "God said to Abraham: 'As for Sarah your wife … I will bless her and give you a son [Isaac]; she shall be the mother of nations. … Then Abraham fell upon his face and laughed, and said in his heart: 'Shall a child be born to him who is 100 years old … and can Sarah bear [a child] who is 90 years old?' … [And God replied] 'Sarah shall bear you a son indeed; and you shall call his name Isaac …'" Genesis 17:15-17

The name "Isaac" literally means "he laughs." When Sarah heard of this coming event, she like Abraham, also laughed.

> "The Lord [then] said to Abraham: 'Why did Sarah laugh …? Is anything too hard for the Lord?'" Genesis 18:13-14

That is the precise point! <u>Is anything too hard for God?</u> Later, the prophet Jeremiah will answer this question.

> "God, you have made the heavens and the earth by your great power ... there is nothing too hard for you." Jeremiah 32:1

In the NT, a similar experience is recorded of Mary and Elizabeth. Elizabeth conceived John the Baptist when she was old. The angel Gabriel spoke of this miracle when appearing to Mary. The angel said:

> "Look at your cousin Elizabeth, who has conceived a son [John] in her old age, and is now in her sixth month [of pregnancy]; who had been [earlier] called 'barren!'" Luke 1:36

The angel spoke these words to Mary who was a virgin and had become pregnant with Jesus. This presented a question for Mary because she had not had any contact with a man.

> "Mary said to the angel: 'How can this be, since I know not a man?' And the angel an-

swered her: 'The Holy Spirit will come upon you, and the power of the Most High [Father] shall overshadow you. Therefore the holy One being born shall be called the Son of God [Jesus].'" Luke 1:34

And then the angel used words very similar to those used by God in his answer to Abraham.

"For nothing will be impossible with God!" Luke 1:37

This statement and the one in Genesis apply to the Holy Eucharist. In the Eucharist, God is making himself appear within an improbable set of material conditions. The bread and wine do not appear to be a proper receptacle for God's Presence. Sarah, Elizabeth, and Mary likewise did not appear to be proper receptacles for human life. Sarah and Elizabeth were "dried up" and Mary's situation was unique. Like the Eucharist at Mass, each was an example of the fact that: "nothing is impossible with God!" If God can create the universe out of nothing, he can surely transform bread and wine into his own "flesh and blood" self!

4.

Melchizedek: Priest Using Bread and Wine

Lot was the nephew of Abraham [Genesis 11:27]. Lot, whose father had died in Ur, moved to Haran in northern Mesopotamia [Genesis 11:28-31]. Later, Lot traveled from Haran to Canaan with Abraham [Genesis 12:5]. In Canaan, Abraham settled in Hebron, a town in the hill country, about 19 miles south of Jerusalem [Genesis 13:18]. Lot eventually settled in the town of Sodom in the valley of the Jordan River [Genesis 13:8-12].

The Jordan Valley was an attractive piece of land for herdsmen like Lot. However, its riches were also attractive to foreign kings. One of these foreign kings was Chedorlaomer who, with three other city-based kings, captured Sodom. They took its treasures and some of its wealthy citizens as prisoners, including Lot [Genesis 14:1-12]. When Abraham heard of this he gathered an army of 318 men and rescued Lot from the outlaw kings [Genesis 14:13-16]. When Abraham returned home he was greeted by Melchizedek, the king of Salem [today's Jerusalem] who was also a priest.

> "Melchizedek, king of [Jeru]Salem, brought out bread and wine; he was a priest of the most high God. And he [Melchizedek] blessed him [Abraham] and said: 'Blessed be Abraham of the most high God, who possesses heaven and earth ... who has delivered your enemies into your hand.' And he [Abraham] gave to him [Melchizedek] a tithe [one-tenth] of all [the booty he had acquired in the battle?] ... And Abraham said:... 'I have lifted up my hand to Yahweh, the most high God, the possessor of heaven and earth.'" Genesis 14:18-22

Melchizedek and Abraham worshipped the same God. Furthermore, Abraham recognized the role of Melchizedek as a priest of this God. Psalm 110:4 would later speak of some priests, as being "of the order of Melchizedek." The job of priests was then, as it is now, to offer gifts. On some occasions, these gifts were intended to "give thanks." Priests often sacrificed animals to make this gift of "thanks" palpable.

However, here Melchizedek brings out bread and wine! Was this bread and wine just a lunch for Abraham, or was it a sacrificial meal? Many scholars relate Melchizedek's bread and wine to the bread and wine of Christ at the Last Supper [Luke 22:19 and 1 Corinthians 11:23-26].

The letter to the "Hebrews" in the NT pushes this comparison even further. It says that there was no genealogy for Melchizedek, no origins. This fact, Hebrew's concludes, was also true of the Son of God [Jesus], who is eternal. Then too there was no record of death for Melchizedek. Like Jesus, the text implies that Melchizedek continues to live forever. Hence Hebrew's concludes that both Melchizedek and Jesus are holding the priesthood forever.

> "This Melchizedek, king of [Jeru]salem, priest of the most high God ... To whom Abraham gave a tenth part ... [was] without father, without mother, without [any] descent; having neither beginning of days [like Jesus], nor end of life [like Jesus]; but was made like the Son of God [Jesus]; abiding as a priest continually." Hebrews 7:1-3

"Meeting of Abraham and Melchizedek"
Dieric Bouts the Elder, 1464–1467
Courtesy of Wikipedia

5.

Joseph and Jesus – on Bread

Jacob was the grandson of Abraham in the Old Testament. Joseph was one of the twelve sons of Jacob. Jacob's name was later changed to "Israel." The twelve sons of the young Jacob eventually formed the "twelve tribes of Israel."

What ties Joseph and Jesus together is the fact that both men were "saviors." Joseph was able to supply the twelve Israeli tribes with grain for bread during a time of famine and thus save them from starvation and death. Jesus was able to supply the world with a new kind of Bread, namely himself, and thereby save those who would receive him from eternal death.

Joseph and Jesus shared some other life identities that would make their likeness even more exact.

[1] Joseph was sold into slavery by his jealous brothers. Jesus came into the world as a kind of slave.

"They [Joseph's brothers] drew Joseph up out of the pit [a dry water well]; and sold Joseph to the Ishmaelites for 20 pieces of silver; who then took Joseph as a slave into Egypt." Genesis 37:28

"Christ Jesus, being in the form of God ... took upon himself the form of a slave [here on earth], and was made in the likeness of man." Philippians 2:5-7

[2] Both Joseph and Jesus were taken into Egypt when young.

"They took Joseph as a slave into Egypt." Genesis 37:28

"He [Jesus' foster father] arose, and took the young child [Jesus] and his mother [Mary] by night, and departed unto Egypt." Matthew 2:14

[3] Both Joseph and Jesus were sold for a few silver coins.

"They … sold Joseph … for 20 pieces of silver." Genesis 37:28

"Judas Iscariot went to the chief priests and said … 'I will deliver him [Jesus] to you; and they weighed him 30 pieces of silver." Matthew 26:15

[4] Later, in Egypt, Joseph rose in position, becoming the Pharaoh's prime minister [Gen 41:39-45]. In the NT, Christ was like a prime minister, representing God the Father in this world, revealing the Father's Word and work.

"You [Joseph] shall be over my house [Pharaoh's kingdom] and according to your word shall all my people be ruled; only on the throne will I [Pharaoh] be greater. And Pharaoh said to Joseph: 'See, I have set you over all the land of Egypt." Genesis 41:39-40

"I [Jesus] manifested your name [Father] to the men whom you gave me." John 17:6

"The word which you hear [on earth from
me] is not mine; but [is rather] the Father's
who sent me [Jesus]." John 14:24

[5] Joseph stored up enough grain in Egyptian gran-
aries to feed not only the Egyptian people in their
time of famine, but also the hungry people of Israel.

Christ, like Joseph, will save his family, the Church,
by providing it with bread – the Bread of his own
Presence.

"Bread was not in all the land [being farmed];
the famine was very severe." Genesis 47:13

"Joseph nourished his father [Jacob] and his
[eleven] brothers and all his father's house
with bread." Genesis 47:12

"You [in the Church] are ... members of the
family of God." Ephesians 2:19

"I [Jesus] am the bread of [eternal] life, the
one coming to me by no means hungers."
John 6:3

[6] Joseph and Jesus were both "saviors." This was the great plan of Yahweh, God the Father. Joseph would nearly die in a dry well, then be taken into Egypt where he would rise to prominence and eventually save Israel from starvation. Jesus would die on the cross, then rise from the dead, to save the New Israel, the Church – initially being led by 12 Apostles who mirrored the 12 sons of Jacob.

> "I am Joseph [the prime minister] whom you [my brothers] sold into Egypt ... do not be grieved ... because you sold me here; for God sent me before you to save [your] life... God sent me before you to put a remnant [of food] in the land, and to keep [Israel] alive; a great deliverance [from death]." Genesis 45:4-7

> "This [my Presence] is the bread that comes down out of Heaven; that anyone may eat of it and may not die. I [Jesus] am the living Bread, the [one] having come down out of Heaven ... the Bread which I will give is my Flesh for the [eternal] life of the world." John 6:50-51

A person is made of "flesh and blood." So too Christ. He gives his Presence personally, as flesh [in the transformed Bread] and as blood [in the transformed Wine]. He transforms the bread and wine to become himself, an invisible Presence in the Eucharist. His Presence within us is our eternal Food [John 6:53 and 55].

"Burning Bush"
Sébastien Bourdon (mid-17th century)
from Hermitage Museum, Saint Petersburg.
Courtesy of Wikipedia.

6.

God of the Burning Bush

In the early days of mankind's stay on this planet, sacrifice was thought to be the proper way to approach God. A lamb, or some other valuable animal, was burned "up" in a fire to satisfy the imagined demands of the gods or God. Fire was the method of removing the animal from this world or of making the animal become invisible to reach God. The smoke and the smell was at the same time thought to migrate upward as a way of communicating with the deity.

Then about 1450 BC, Moses was tending sheep in the land of Midian, north of Egypt, when he saw an unusual fire (1 Kings 6:1). This was not a sacrificial fire or even an ordinary fire, since it burned on and on without consuming the bush wherein it was located. When Moses approached to examine this unusual sight, "the Angel of Yahweh" appeared to him within the fire [Exodus 3:2]. The Angel of Yahweh told Moses to take off his shoes since he was standing upon "holy ground." This situation involved a Heavenly Person, not consumed by fire.

> "God called to him out of the midst of the [burning] bush." Exodus 3:4

A conversation thereafter ensued between Moses and God. Moses was told by this "Word of God" Presence to go into Egypt and free the Hebrew people who were enslaved. This slavery was both physical and spiritual. The Hebrews in Egypt were beginning to follow the Egyptian gods, and Yahweh, God the Father, wanted this to end. He wanted to free both the body and the soul of the Hebrews in Egypt.

Moses, of course, wanted to know more about this God who was speaking to him. So he asked the name of the God within the fire. To this question he was given the Name: "I Am Who I Am." This God said further: " ... you shall say that 'I Am' has sent me to you" [Exodus 3:14].

Moses thereafter went into Egypt, and God simultaneously brought judgment or ten "plagues" upon the gods of Egypt. Moses then led the Hebrew slaves out of Egypt and eventually into the Promised Land which would later be called "Israel."

The identity of Jesus, as the same God present in the "burning bush" of the Exodus, is seen within the "I Am" statements of Jesus. In these statements Jesus uses the Name of God given in the "burning bush" of Moses' experience. They clarify Jesus' identity and mission. His mission on earth is to free mankind from its worship of false gods [Satan, sex, money, power, the world … as in Egypt] and to lead all persons out of this world and into the true Promised Land of Heaven.

Here are some of the "I Am" statements of Jesus, tying him directly to the "burning bush" of the Exodus.

"Be of good cheer, I Am … be not afraid." Mark 6:50 and Matt 14:27

"When you lift up the Son of Man [onto the cross], you will know that I Am." John 8:28

"Before Abraham was, I Am." John 8:58 [see Exodus 3:6]

"I Am the light of the world [in the burning bush]." John 9:5

There are three "I Am" statements of Jesus that connect directly to the Eucharist and to the Mass.

"I Am the Bread of life." John 6:35

"I Am the Bread, the One coming down from Heaven." John 6:41

"I Am the Bread, the living One from Heaven. Whoever eats of this Bread will live forever." John 6:51

"The Angel of Death and the First Passover" from illustrators of the 1897 Bible Pictures and What They Teach Us by Charles Foster. Courtesy of Wikipedia.

7.

Passover & Idolatry

When God revealed himself to Moses from within the "burning bush" he said: "'I am the God of Abraham, the God of Isaac, and the God of Jacob.' And Moses hid his face; for he was afraid to look upon God." Exodus 3:6

This event occurred about 1450 BC. Abraham, Isaac, and Jacob had lived about 430 years earlier [Exodus 12:40]. This one God, Yahweh, already had a long history among the Hebrew people. Yet, in Egypt, the native people still worshipped gods and goddesses. Yahweh sent Moses into Egypt to correct this situation and to remove the Hebrew people from Egyptian idolatry and slavery.

> "They sacrificed to devils [evil angels], and not to God ... to gods whom they knew not." Deuteronomy 32:17

God would first warn the Egyptian people with a series of "plagues." For example, the Egyptians worshiped the Nile River, as the people in India today worship the Ganges River as the goddess "Ganga." God, therefore, turned the Nile River into a blood-like liquid [Exodus 17:20]. They also worshiped "Hecker," the frog god. So God caused an infestation of frogs over the land [Exodus 8:6]. They worshiped the bull god "Apis" and the cow god "Hathor." So God killed Egyptian livestock by plagues of lice, flies, and boils [Ex 8:17 & 24; 9:6 & 10]. They worshiped their kings as gods, so God destroyed the cereal crops of the people with hail and locusts [Ex 9:22 & 10:14]. And for long they had worshiped the sun as the god "Re." So Yahweh darkened their land for three days.

But none of these partial punishments caused a change in Egyptian behavior. The Egyptians continued with their own invented religion. God, therefore, chose a more painful solution. This would involve the first-born sons of Egyptian families. The first-born sons were the religious leaders in the Egyptian religious system. So, God sought to remove these leaders of the false religion.

By comparison, we moderns think that the "enlight-
enment" has moved us beyond any kind of idolatry.
However, there remain several examples. In Asia today, for example, there is Gautama "Buddha" who
lived five centuries before Christ and never claimed
to be anything but a man seeking peace, who is pres-
ently worshiped. Hinduism is a pantheistic religion
still active in the world. It teaches that the universe is
God: "the One that is the all." The human person is
said to be a part of this "All." However, in spite of such
assertions, Hinduism also has its own major gods.
They are three: Brahma, Vishnu, and Shiva. And
there are numerous lesser Hindu gods that are viewed
simply as "incarnations" of the three main deities.
"Krishna" is said to be one of the incarnated Hindu
gods. The Ganges River is also said to be a reincarna-
tion of the goddess "Ganga."

Islam was invented in the 7th century after Christ by
Mohammed. It adopted a god from the Arabian Pen-
insula named "Allah," who was inserted by Mohammed into Bible history. The major characters of the
Bible [Adam, Noah, Abraham, Moses, David Solomon, and Jesus] are all presented within the Quran as

preachers of Allah. And to make this work, much of the Bible that existed before Mohammed was said to be a lie!

For example, Jesus was said not to be divine, but only a man who preached Allah. Furthermore, Jesus was said not to have died on the cross, or to have been raised from the dead! The Quran says that Allah simply took Jesus up into one of his seven heavens; the exact one is not stated.

Mormonism is another man-made religion with idols. Its founder, Joseph Smith, claimed to have received an angelic vision telling him the location of golden plates [now lost] containing God's revelation. This, he published in 1830, as the Book of Mormon. Smith accepted the Bible, but like Mohammed, diverged greatly from its teachings.

And so it goes! Man in his many ways refuses to follow the God who revealed himself in history – the God of the Bible. In the example of Egypt, the first-born sons furthered the worship of Egypt's various gods and goddesses. To stop this affront to God, the event known as the Passover came into being. Rebellious Egyptian families would lose their first-born sons to help terminate Egypt's idolatry. The first-born sons of Hebrew families would be spared if they followed specific instructions given by God. Moses was told that Hebrew families had to sacrifice a lamb to the one true God of Abraham and Isaac. This had to be done following the steps laid out in Exodus 12:1-28. The lamb had to be without blemish. Its blood [believed to be its life] had to be placed upon the frame of the front door of each Hebrew house. The lamb had to have no broken bones, and it had to be completely eaten as a meal. The bread eaten with the lamb had to be unleavened, a sign of haste [Leviticus 23:4-6]. Furthermore, the Hebrew family had to be standing and dressed so as to be ready to "exit" Egypt. And this ritual event had to be repeated each year in all generations.

The primary concern behind the Passover ritual was idolatry. And behind the worship of idols were rebellious angels that God had removed from Heaven. These wicked angels or devils [demons] were very efficient at leading humans into false paths of worship.

They helped humans make wrong decisions about who God is. Their leader, Satan, himself sought to be worshiped. This is why he was removed from Heaven.

> "War broke out in Heaven. Michael and his angels fought against the dragon [Satan]. The dragon and his angels fought back, but they were defeated and there was no longer a place for them in Heaven. The great dragon was thrown down, that ancient serpent, who is called the Devil or Satan, the deceiver of the whole world." Revelation 12:7-9

On earth, Satan and his followers attempt to lead every person astray. Idolatry is one of their primary goals. Satan is supremely confident, even to the point of tempting Jesus himself.

> "The tempter [Satan] said to him [Jesus]: 'If you are the Son of God command these stones [in the desert] to become loaves of bread.' But he [Jesus] answering said: 'It has been written that man does not live on bread

alone, but on every word that comes from the mouth of God.'" Matthew 4:3-4

This passage contains an outline of the Catholic Mass – in reverse. It speaks of the liturgy of the Word [1]:Man needing "every word that comes from the mouth of God." And then [2] it speaks of the liturgy of the Eucharist: "Command these [bread-like] stones [one reality] to become loaves of bread [another reality]." If Jesus had done this it would have been analogous to changing bread at Mass into his own Body [Luke 22:19].

"Mystic Lamb"
Jan van Eyck (1432)
Courtesy of Wikipedia

8.

Lamb of God

Each year the "Passover feast" remembers the beginnings of the "exodus" of the Hebrew slaves and their families out of Egypt. This Exodus of a large number of people from Egypt eventually ended in their occupation of the land of Canaan [what is today the nation of Israel]. The Exodus began about 1446 BC (1 Kings 6:1).

The Passover ritual for this feast is set forth in the Book of Exodus 12:1-14. In the instructions, Moses was told by God that each Hebrew family would be saved if they sacrificed a lamb to the one true God of Abraham and Isaac. This had to be done very precisely. The lamb had to be without blemish. Its blood [believed to be its life] had to be put on the frame of the front door of each house. The lamb had to have no broken bones. It had to be roasted and eaten. And the family had to be dressed and ready to "exit" Egypt.

If these tasks were completed God would "pass-over" the Hebrew house. There would be no death within the house of the obedient family. God would then lead the Hebrews out of Egypt and provide them with Manna [a bread-like food] until they had arrived in the Promised Land of Canaan [today's Israel].

All these Passover details would later shed light upon the work of Christ. In the NT, Christ is the Passover Lamb, the one who gives eternal life to those who receive him within a sacred meal – the Mass. Like the Passover lamb, he is unblemished. He is perfect: having no sin. He dies during Passover. Not a bone of his body would be broken. Every Christian must eat his body, the consecrated Bread of Mass, to be saved [Matt 26:26; John 6:53]. By consuming his Blood [or life] under the appearance of consecrated Wine, Christians would be given eternal life. Christians are thereafter to dress themselves in love-works, exiting this world on the way to Heaven: "Faith works by love." Galatians 5:6

1. "In the first month of the [Jewish] new year [is Passover]." Ex 12:2

NT "It was Passover … and they … sought to seize him [Christ] … that they might kill him [as the Passover Lamb]." Mark 14:1

"I [Christ] desire to eat this Passover with you before I suffer." Lk 22:15

2. "Take … one lamb for a house." Ex 12:3

NT "Behold the lamb of God [Christ]." Jn 1:29

3. "The lamb [is to be] a perfect one." Ex 12:5

NT "Christ … did not sin." 1 Pt 2:22

"[Christ was] undefiled, separated from sinners." Heb 7:26

4. "On the 14th day kill it [the lamb] …" Ex 12:6

NT "Christ our Passover was sacrificed." 1 Cor 5:7

"I saw in the midst of the throne [in Heaven]
… a Lamb [the Christ] standing as having
been slain …" Rev 3:7

5. "Put its blood on two doorposts and lintel … take
a bunch of hyssop, dip it in the [lamb's] blood and
strike the lintel [beam above the door]." Ex 12:22

NT "On the cross they filled a sponge with
vinegar [red wine soured] and put it upon
hyssop and put it to his [Christ's] mouth." Jn
19:20

6. "You shall not fracture a bone from it [the Passover
lamb]." Ex 12:46

NT "When they [the Roman soldiers] came
to Jesus, and saw that he was already dead
they did not break his legs." Jn 19:33

7. "They shall eat the [roasted] flesh on this night …
leave not any of it [uneaten]." Ex 12:8f

NT "Having taken bread, Jesus said: 'Take, eat: this [consecrated Bread] is my Body.'" Matt 26:26

8. "Eat it with your loins girded [ready to leave]." Ex 12:11

NT "Let your loins be girded and your lamps burning; and you will be like men awaiting [the coming of] the Lord." Lk 12:35-36

9. "I [God] will pass through Egypt … this night." Ex 12:12

NT "The day of the Lord comes as a thief in the night." 1 Thess 5:4

10. "I will … smite every first-born in Egypt …" Ex 12:12

NT "He [Jesus] is the first-born from the dead." Col 1:18

11. "The blood shall be a sign for you on your houses … I [God] will see the blood, and I will pass over you…" Ex 12:13

> NT "They overcame him [Satan] because of the blood of the Lamb." Rev 12:11

> "By his [Jesus'] blood, we shall be saved." Ro 5:9

> "In him we have redemption by his blood, the forgiveness of transgressions, in accord with the riches of his grace." Eph 1:7

12. "This day [Passover] shall be a memorial for you …" Ex 12:14a

> NT "Taking a loaf [of bread] and having given thanks, he [Christ] broke it, and gave it to them saying: 'This is my Body for you being given. This do you for my remembrance'" [or memorial)]. Lk 22:19

13. "You shall celebrate it [the Passover] as a feast to God ... forever you shall celebrate it." Ex 12:14b

> NT "Christ, our Passover was celebrated, so let us keep the feast [forever] ..." 1 Cor 5:7-8

> "The Lamb [Christ] is Lord" Rev 17:14

> "Blessed are the ones called to the supper of the Lamb." Rev 19:9

The apostle Paul taught the Gospel message in the city of Corinth during the years 51 and 52 AD. He then wrote back to them, 1 Corinthians, probably in 53 AD. In this letter, he says that Christ is the new Passover Lamb and that Christians should "keep the feast" [1 Corinthians 5:7-8]. But how would this be done and when? In 1 Corinthians 11:23-24 Paul explains how. He repeats the instructions of Jesus at the Last Supper: "The Lord Jesus ... took bread and having given thanks [using his intention], broke it and said: 'This is my [Passover] Body: do this in remembrance of me." To "do this" means that Christians are to use the very words and intentions of Christ because they are powerful. One example of this is embedded in creation: "Let there be light! And there was light" [Genesis 1:3]. Paul goes on to say that after this Passover action, Christians are to be discerning of the Presence of the Lord's Body [1 Corinthians 11:29]. He further says that not to see Jesus in the Communion Bread is to bring "judgment" upon one's self. Finally, Paul counsels frequent Communion: "as often as you eat this bread and drink this cup, you declare the [Passover] death of the Lord [Jesus] until he comes [again]" [1 Corinthians 11:26].

9.

Remembering

In the Old Testament, after the Passover was completed, the Hebrew slaves exited Egypt and began their journey to the promised land of Canaan [later renamed "Israel"].

This Exodus people were told early on by Moses to never forget their God, Yahweh, who had saved them from slavery and idolatry in Egypt. They were told not only to "remember" the Passover events but to re-enact them each year as a "memorial" feast. This feast would be named "Passover" and would last a full seven days.

What follows will be an excursion into OT and NT scripture. First, the discipline of "remembering" will be examined in the OT at large. Second, the commands to "memorialize" the OT Passover events will be presented. Third, the NT statement of Christ "to remember" his transformation of bread and wine during the Last Supper will be presented.

First, there is the seriousness of remembering agreements made with God, together with his accompanying promises. These agreements with God are called "covenants," and they are ever present within the OT. Jesus would later speak of a "New Covenant" during his Last Supper with the Apostles [Luke 22:20]. It is also called the "New Testament."

"Remember Abraham, Isaac, and Jacob, my servants … I [God] will multiply their seed as the stars of heaven, and all the land [of Israel] … I give to your seed [offspring], and they shall inherit it forever." Exodus 32:13

> "Remember the word which Moses the servant of the Lord commanded you, saying: 'The Lord your God has given you … this land.'" Joshua 1:13

> "Your burnt offerings and … peace offerings shall be a memorial for you before your God." Numbers 10:10

"I will make your name [God] to be remembered in all generations ... the people will praise you forever and ever." Psalm 45:17

"I will remember the works of the Lord. Surely I will remember your wonders of old. I will meditate on all of your work, and talk of your doings." Psalm 77:11-12

"Seek the Lord and his strength: seek his face evermore. Remember his marvelous works that he has done." Psalm 105:4-5

"You [are] the seed of Abraham his servant; you [are] children of Jacob, his chosen ... He has remembered his covenant forever; the word which he commanded to a thousand generations. The covenant he made with Abraham, and his oath to Isaac; and confirmed the same unto Jacob for a law ... an everlasting covenant: saying, 'Unto you will I give the land of Canaan.'" Psalm 105:6-11

During the OT Passover, Moses was told by God, to "memorialize" its events. This was not meant to be a simple "remembering" of the Passover; but rather a re-living or re-enactment of the events leading up to the Exodus out of Egypt. It was to be a "memorial" celebrated from generation to generation. Exodus 12:14 makes this very clear. This Passover feast was to be seven days in length.

> "This day shall be unto you for a memorial; and you shall keep it as a feast to the Lord throughout [all] your generations. You shall keep it a feast by an ordinance forever." Exodus 12:14

> "When your children shall say to you: 'What do you mean by this service?' You shall say: 'It is the sacrifice of the Lord's Passover, who passed over the houses of the children of Israel in Egypt, when he smote the Egyptians.'" Exodus 12:26-27

> "Moses said to the people: 'Remember this day, in which you came out from Egypt ... by the strength of the hand of the Lord [who] brought you out from that place.'" Exodus 13:3

"Seven days you shall eat unleavened [flat] bread, and on the seventh day there shall be a [second] feast to the Lord … And you shall show your son [in all generations], saying: 'This is done because of that which the Lord did to me when I [speedily] came forth out of Egypt. And it shall be … for a memorial.'" Exodus 13:6-9

Finally, there is the Passover revealed in the NT. This Passover is referred to as the Last Supper.

"I [Jesus] have desired to eat this Passover with you [the Last Supper] before I suffer." Luke 22:16

At this Passover meal Jesus revealed a divine action of awesome proportions. He revealed the new method of providing a lamb for future Passover feasts. That lamb would be himself: the Lamb of God, called into Presence upon an altar by priestly prayer.

The following are the words of institution that he gave the Church. In these words of institution, it is important to recognize that Jesus did not say either: [1]

This is a symbol of my Body [Calvin], or [2] This is my Body within the bread [Luther]. Jesus said rather that: This is my Body [the Catholic reading]. The bread continues to look like bread and to taste like bread, but Jesus said it would truly be his very own Body. This is the same divine Person who had earlier said: "Let there be light!" and there was light [Genesis 1:3]. And who instantaneously changed about 120 gallons of water into wine at Cana [John 2:6-9]. God is powerful! And he cannot lie [Numbers 23:19; Titus 1:2]. Does anyone understand how God could do these things? No. Will it ever be understood? No. But he did them! Do physicists understand how "gluons," particles without mass, hold neutrons and protons together inside the atomic nucleus? No. But they do!

Believers must be like children in this respect. Children tend to believe everything that their father or mother tells them. Christians are counseled by Christ to do the same [Mark 10:5].

Twenty years after Jesus died as the Passover Lamb upon a cross near Jerusalem and then rose from the dead, St. Paul went to Corinth in Greece to share the "good news" with its people. He taught the gospel message in Corinth during the years 51-52 AD. This is known because Paul was forced by certain Jews to appear before the Roman judge, "Gallio" [Acts 18:11-17]. Gallio's "judgment seat" was later found in the ruins of Corinth. Furthermore, an inscription concerning Gallio was uncovered at Delphi which put him in Corinth as judge between 51-52 AD. Gallio's brother, the philosopher Seneca, was a teacher of Emperor Nero [emperor between 54-68 AD].

After Paul left Corinth he wrote two letters to his new church in Corinth. The first of these letters was probably written in 53 AD. In this letter he repeats almost word for word what Jesus told his apostles at the Last Supper in Luke 22:19.

"I [Paul] have received from the Lord [Jesus, who appeared to him – Acts 9:3-5] that which I also delivered to you [in 51 AD]: That the Lord Jesus ... took bread and when he had given thanks [with intention], he broke it, and said: 'Take, eat: this is my Body which is broken for you: do this [same action] in <u>remembrance of me</u>.'" 1 Cor. 11:23-24

Why would Paul repeat the words: "Do this in remembrance of me," twenty years after Jesus said
them? In the first place, Mass was being celebrated in
"home churches" within the Roman Empire in many
places by 53 AD. They were doing, or re-enacting,
what Jesus had said for them to do. But how do we
know this to be true? The answer is that Paul specifically tells us of this fact in this same letter! Look at 1
Corinthians 11:28-30 just five lines after the very
words of Jesus at the Last Supper are laid out by Paul.
"Let a man examine himself, and so let him eat of the
bread and drink of the cup [of wine]. For he that eats
and drinks unworthily, eats and drinks Judgment to
himself, [because he is] not discerning the Lord's
Body. Because of this [lack of belief] many among
you are weak and sick, and [in fact] many [have al-
ready] died." 1 Cor 11:28-30

Paul does not mean to say that this divine Presence of
Jesus happened only once at the Last Supper, or that
it is now happening again in 53 AD in Corinth. Rather he implies that it has been happening for twenty
years. In this regard Paul offers two other statements
that are worth pondering.

> "For as <u>often</u> as you eat this bread [trans-
> formed] and drink this cup [of wine trans-
> formed], you show the Lord's death [at Mass]
> until he comes [at the end of time]." 1 Cor
> 11:26

The second text worth pondering is Paul's admoni-
tion to continue the Passover celebration, as counseled by God in Exodus 12:14.

> Paul: "Christ our Passover [Lamb] was sacri-
> ficed [in Jerusalem], so let us [now continue
> to] keep the [new Passover] feast." 1 Cor 5:7-
> 8

In other words the Passover feast of the new era has
been celebrated for twenty years. Paul says: Let's
"keep" it going! Our Passover Lamb is Christ, the
eternal One.

10.

Manna – Bread for 5000 - Eucharist

1. OT Manna

The Hebrew people of the Exodus had two immediate life-threatening problems. One was the need for water to hydrate their bodies, and the other was a need for a reliable source of food. In the desert-like environment of the Wilderness, these became significant problems. The first, however, was solved by "the Rock" that followed them according to Paul, who was Christ [1 Corinthians 10:4]. From his position in the cloud the Lord Jesus made the Hebrew leaders stop at exactly the correct places for the necessary water [Exodus 13:21].

The second problem was more difficult. The Hebrews had been accustomed to a wide variety of foods, grown along the Nile River in Egypt. In the desert, they saw few things growing and even fewer that they could eat. Certainly, a considerable number of people, such as the Twelve Hebrew tribes of Israel, could not be sustained by desert plants alone. There was, for example, one kind of food generated by insects feeding on the sap of "tamarisk" bushes. However, this would not have been extensive enough to feed large numbers of people. Also certain birds such as quail migrated through the area at different times of the year, but this also was a limited food source. The Hebrew people early on became hungry and needed food. They "murmured" among themselves and eventually attacked Moses with abusive language. So, Moses took his worries to God who offered a solution. God would give his people a new kind of food called "Manna." This food would be found each morning on the ground like the dew-fall. About two quarts for each person would be collected. And God would miraculously provide this food for all the Hebrew travelers until they entered Canaan. That would be for forty years!

> "In the morning you shall be satisfied with bread; and you shall know that I am Yahweh your God ... and in the morning there was a layer of dew around the camp. And as the layer of dew went up [evaporated] on the face of the wilderness there was a small scale-like

substance ... and Moses said to them: 'This is the bread which Yahweh has given to you for food." Exodus 16:12-16

"Israel called its name 'Manna.' It was the seed of white coriander, and its taste was like cakes of honey ... and the sons of Israel ate the Manna 40 years until their coming into the inhabited land   ... the border of the land of Canaan." Exodus 16:31; 35-36

The Book of Numbers explains that the Manna was crushed and then boiled to make little cakes.

"The Manna was like coriander seed, and its look like that of bdellium [a resin gum]. And the people gathered it and ground it in mills or beat it in mortars, and boiled it in a pan, and then made it into cakes." Numbers 11:7-8

Psalm 78 describes how the Manna came down from heaven like rain. In the NT, Jesus would explain that he too had come down from Heaven to give a special kind of life to the world: eternal or everlasting life.

"He [God] opened the doors of the heavens,
and he rained on them Manna to eat. The
grain of the heavens he gave to them. The
bread of the mighty man did eat." Psalm
78:23-25

"The Bread of God is the one coming down
out of Heaven [Christ] and gives [eternal] life
to the world." John 6:33

"I [Christ] am the Bread of life ... I have come
down from Heaven." John 6:35, 41

"I [Christ] am the living Bread, the one out of
Heaven having come down. If anyone eats of
this Bread, he will live to the age [forever];
and the Bread which I will give is my Flesh
[the Eucharist] for the life of the world." John
6:51

2. NT Manna

During his public ministry, Jesus miraculously multiplied bread on at least two occasions, to feed many
thousands of people. One of these miracles became

known as the "Feeding of the 5000." The number 5000 referred only to men; with women and children it could have been 20,000. Each of the four gospel accounts report this miracle [Matt 14:17-21; Mark 6:38-44; Luke 9:13-17; John 6:9-14].

The Book of John begins at 6, 4 saying that this miracle occurred "near the Passover"; thus recalling the Exodus out of Egypt and the feeding of the twelve tribes of Israel with the "Manna."

Before this miracle proceeded, the apostles gave Jesus five loaves of bread and two fish. With these starters, 5-20,000 people were miraculously fed. The food was multiplied, and when everyone was full, the apostles picked up 12 baskets of fragments [Matt 14:20; Mk 6:43; Luke 9:17; John 6:13].

> "Then they gathered them together, and filled twelve baskets with the fragments of the five barley loaves, which remained over and above that which they [the people] had eaten. Then when they had seen what miracle Jesus had done, they said: 'This [Jesus] is of truth that

prophet [a new Moses] who should come into
the world.'" John 6:13-14

The 12 baskets of leftovers meant that each of the 12
apostles, or early bishops, would have a basketful of
Christ to distribute to a "tribe" of believers. Christ
would be the New Manna from Heaven which would
feed the 12 tribes of the New Israel, the Church. This
group, the Twelve, was an "organ" within the Church.
Apostolic members, like Judas, were replaced [Acts
1:20-26]. Such lists of ordained bishops existed by the
early second century. Irenaeus, bishop of Lyon,
France [140-202 AD] lists the bishops of Rome in his
book "Against Heresies" Book III, 3.3.

A common belief in the 1st century was that when
the Messiah came he would renew the sending of
Manna from heaven. He would behave as Moses had
done in the OT [Deuteronomy 18:15]. However, they
were not sure about Jesus since Moses, they thought,
had fed the whole people, not once, but for forty
years. Furthermore, while Jesus had multiplied ordinary bread, Moses had given them "bread from
Heaven" [Psalm 78:24].

3. Manna: Bread that perishes

The day after Jesus miraculously fed the 5000 [families?], he and his apostles arrived in Capernaum and were met by the same crowds. These people wanted more of the bread that Jesus had given them the previous day. Jesus knew this and said:

> "You seek me not because you saw the miracles [his many miracles], but because you ate the loaves [of bread] and were filled. Work not for [earthly] food which does not last, but for the food which endures to eternal [everlasting] life; which the Son of Man [myself in Daniel 7:13] will give to you." John 6:26-27

These same people remembered that, as they understood it, Moses had given them "bread from heaven" for a full forty years, and so they challenged Jesus.

> "What sign do you show [us now] that we can see and believe in you? ... Our [OT] fathers ate Manna in the desert ... bread from heaven was provided." John 6:30-31

Jesus then, presented them with the truth about this Manna. He said that the result of eating ordinary bread, such as Manna, was that it would not last. Hunger would return, and eventually even death would overtake them.

> "Then Jesus said to them ... "Moses did not give you that bread from heaven [the Manna]; rather my Father [did] ... Work not for the [kind of] food which is being destroyed." John 6:33 & 27

> "Your [OT] fathers did eat Manna in the Wilderness, and are [all] dead." John 6:49

4. <u>Jesus: Living Bread from Heaven</u>

Jesus went on to reveal the kind of bread that offers everlasting life for the world, namely himself. He is the true "Bread from Heaven."

> "The Bread of God is the one who comes down from Heaven and gives [eternal] life to the world. They [the people] then said to him: 'Lord, give us this bread [as Moses did] al-

ways.' Jesus [then] said to them: 'I Am the Bread of life; the one coming to me will never hunger [again], and the one trusting in me will never thirst [again].'" John 6:33-35

The Jews present began "grumbling" because Jesus had said: "I Am the Bread … who comes down from Heaven." This grumbling resembled the "murmuring" of the Hebrews on the Exodus when they were short of food [Exodus 6:12].

The one who eats at Christ's table will never hunger again because of Christ's real Presence in the Eucharist, the divinized Bread.

"I Am the Bread of life. Your ancestors ate Manna in the desert, and they died. This [Eucharist] is the Bread that comes down from Heaven, so that some might eat of it and not die." John 6:48-50

5. Jesus speaks of the Last Supper

In John 6, Jesus will describe the consecrated Bread of the Last Supper as "his Flesh … for the life of the world." The "Judeans" present at the time responded by asking themselves the following question: "How is this man able to give us his flesh to eat?" We too would have asked this question had we been there! However, Jesus would not explain the "how" to them at that particular time. He would rather choose to answer that question at the Last Supper itself when he consecrated bread and wine and explained the meaning of his actions for the apostles. At this moment, Jesus spoke of the utter reality of his eternal gift for the world. His point was that the word "Flesh" meant his Body, and the word "Blood" meant his eternal life. In other words, he is giving the world his Flesh and Blood self, his Flesh and Blood Presence.

In the ancient world, one's "life" was thought to reside in the blood.

"The life is in the blood ..." Leviticus 17:11

"Eat not the blood; for the blood is the life." Deut 12:23

Even today, if the blood runs out of a person's body, he dies. Hence, the origin of this belief. Jesus respected ancient traditions; however, his meaning was eternal life.

In the Eucharistic verses of John, one sees the literal emphasis of Jesus. These verses are John 6:51-59.

> "I Am the living Bread which came down from Heaven. If any man eat of this Bread he will live forever; and the Bread that I will give is my Flesh [under the appearance of Bread] which I will give for the [eternal] life of the world ... Except you eat the Flesh of the Son of Man, and drink his Blood [under the appearance of Wine], you have no life in you. Whoever eats my Flesh, and drinks my Blood, has eternal life; and I will raise him up on the last day. For my Flesh is true food, and my Blood is true drink. He that eats my Flesh and drinks my Blood dwells in me and I in him. Just as I [Jesus] live through [God] the Father, so he that eats me [Jesus] shall live by me. This is the Bread that came down from Heaven; not as your ancestors who ate Manna, and are dead; he that eats this Bread shall live forever."
> John 6:51-59

Notice that Jesus used the word "Flesh" five times when referring to his Body. Everyone knew what he meant by these words, because "many of his disciples said: 'This [flesh stuff] is a hard saying; who can hear it?' [John 6:60] However, Jesus did not back down. He did not say: "You misunderstood me! I was speaking symbolically." Rather he said: "What if you see the Son of Man [me] ascend up to where he was before [in Heaven]?" [John 6:62]. And, of course, he would later do this, in his "Ascension" into Heaven [Acts 1:9]. The result?

> "From that time many of his disciples no longer walked with him." John 6:66

Finally, Jesus addressed "the Twelve" apostles [the future "overseers" or bishops]. He said to them: 'Will you also go away?' [John 6:67] Peter, the first Pope, answered for the group, saying No! "Lord, to whom shall we go? You [only] have the words of eternal life." John 6:68

6. Last Supper: Heavenly Bread for All [the Mass]

"How can this man give us his flesh to eat?" That was the question! At the Last Supper, Jesus answered this question. His answer would involve an un-bloody solution. He said that he would transform bread by his powerful word to be his own Body, and he would transform wine by his powerful word, to be his own Blood. Thereafter his "Flesh and Blood" Presence would constitute "Holy Communion" for those present at Mass.

In the first half of Mass, the "liturgy of the Word" presents Jesus' actions and teachings from the Bible. In the second half of the Mass, the "liturgy of the Eucharist" makes possible "Communion" with the Lord. This Presence of the eternal Lord within a communicant points to their eternal life with the Lord. In fact, it begins that Heavenly experience!

"As they were eating [the OT Passover meal – v.18], Jesus took bread, and blessed it, and broke it, and gave it to the disciples, and said: 'Take, eat; this [consecrated Bread] is my Body.' And he took the cup [of red? wine], and

gave thanks, and gave it to them, saying:
'Drink you all of it [the consecrated Wine] for
this is my Blood of the new covenant, which
is shed for many for the remission of sins.'"
Matthew 26:26-28

The Last Supper accounts of Mark [14:22-24], Luke
[22:19-20] and Paul [1 Corinthians 11:23-25] are almost identical, or very similar to that of Matthew.

7. Non-Catholic Reaction

The statement of Jesus saying that: "Unless you eat the
Flesh of the Son of Man and drink his Blood, you
have no [eternal] life in you," receives negative reactions even today. One of the verses, that those who
reject the words of Jesus quote, is John 6:63.

"The spirit is the one making [us] live, the
flesh benefits nothing; the words I have spoken to you are [for the] spirit and are life."
John 6:63

This statement can easily be wrongly understood. Jesus is not saying here that his Flesh profits nothing!

He is rather speaking of flesh [as nature] and spirit [as super nature]. In other words: his kind of food is for the "spirit"; the Eucharist does not profit the "flesh" directly. The following quotations mirror the meaning of John 6:63.

> "The one born from flesh is flesh, and the one born from spirit [or soul] is spirit." John 3:6

> "Make no provision for the flesh." Romans 13:14

> "You are not in the flesh, but in the spirit." Romans 8:9

Another form of rejection of Jesus' statement is to say that one can be saved merely by a simple "belief" in Jesus. Certain passages from within John 6 are used to demonstrate this idea.

> "He that believes in me shall never thirst." John 6:35

"That everyone who sees the Son [Jesus], and
believes in him, may have eternal life." John
6:40

"Amen, amen, I say to you, the one believing
[or trusting in Jesus] has eternal life." John
6:47

Here again questions arise. Can one "believe" in
someone, while at the same time be rejecting what
they say? Does Jesus mean by these words an exterior
belief only? The true believer, to the contrary, wants
to know everything about the person they revere, and
then "follow" that person. Jesus said many times: "follow me!" Here Jesus says: Eat my Flesh and drink my
Blood that you might have eternal life. This statement
must certainly be included in any definition of au-
thentic "belief" in him! And he makes this situation
easy for people: by authorizing the transformation of
bread into his Body, and by authorizing the transformation of wine into his Blood. He said at the Last
Supper: "Do this [action] in remembrance of me"
[Luke 22:19; 1 Corinthians 11:24]. This "un-bloody"
way of ensuring his ongoing "personal" Presence was
really a very kind gesture. We must have faith in his

promises and faith in his power to make this happen. The Eucharist looks like bread, but it is his Body; it looks like wine, but it is his Blood. He is there before us in this ongoing personal way. A divine gift!

Cover Design for The Missing Chalice by Richard C. Hanley
(En Route Books and Media, 2017)
artist, Richard E. Hanley

11.

Water - Wine - Eucharist

After the Passover Meal was completed, the Hebrew slaves and their families exited Egypt about 1446 BC. Once in the desert a new set of challenges faced the Hebrew travelers. They were soon very thirsty in an extremely parched landscape.

> "Moses moved Israel from the Sea of Reeds into the wilderness of Shur; and they went three days into the wilderness and did not find water." Ex. 15:22

God solved this early problem by sweetening the "bitter water" of a water hole called Marah. This miracle temporarily satisfied the Hebrew people [Exodus 15:23-25]. However, the problem of water shortage continued; and when the Hebrews reached Rephidim near Mt. Sinai, Moses began to be abused verbally.

> "Israel … pitched [camp] at Rephidim and there was no water for the people to drink.

And the people fought with Moses ... and Moses said to the people: 'Why do you fight with me? Why do you tempt Yahweh?' ... And Moses cried to Yahweh [God the Father] saying: 'What shall I do to this people? Yet a little while and they will stone me.' And Yahweh said to Moses: 'Go on in front of the people, and take with you the elders of Israel; and in your hand take the [shepherd's] staff with which you struck the Nile [River]. Behold, I will stand there before you on the rock in Horeb, and you shall strike the rock, and water will come out of it and the people will drink.' And Moses did so before the eyes of the elders of Israel." Ex. 17:1-7

Another version of this miracle is recorded in the Book of Numbers.

"Yahweh spoke to Moses, saying: ' ... speak to the rock before their eyes. And it will give its water and you will bring water out of the rock for them' ... Moses lifted his hands and struck the rock twice with his rod; and water came out; and the congregation and their animals drank." Numbers 20:7-11

About 53 AD, the Apostle Paul wrote the following words concerning this water situation on the Exodus.

"All [the people of the Exodus] drank the same spiritual drink; for they drank of a spiritual rock following [them], and that rock was Christ." 1 Corinthians 10:4

What Paul is saying here is that after this miracle, for the entire forty year wilderness journey, the Hebrew people had no problem in finding water. The source of their water was the Lord Jesus himself who traveled with them! Whenever they needed water the Lord found a spot and made it happen. He was the living rock that followed them on their journey and kept them moving. He was the living Water.

How could Paul have identified the solution to this water problem? Where did he get this information about Christ? The answer is that Christ appeared to Paul when he was en route to Damascus in Syria [Acts 9:1-12]. Paul was thrown off his horse and a white cloud appeared before him, not unlike that which the Hebrews followed in their forty year journey across the desert to Canaan. Christ spoke with Paul from within this luminescent cloud, like he had earlier spoken to Moses. He told Paul that he was persecuting Christ, when he persecuted Christians. He may also have told Paul in this conversation how he had rescued the Hebrews in Egypt and provided them with drinking water along the way on their journey to the "promised land" [what later became modern Israel]. Paul may have also spoken to Christ at a later date, for he makes the following statement in 1 Corinthians 11:23: "I [Paul] have received from the Lord that which I also delivered to you: That on the night he was betrayed, the Lord Jesus took bread … etc."

Another way Paul may have recognized the "spiritual rock" as Christ was through his knowledge of the OT Torah. He was a student of the first five books of the Bible. Some passages in the Torah speak of the mysterious cloud that the Hebrews followed on their Wilderness Journey.

> "I [Yahweh] am sending My Angel [literally 'messenger'] before you [Hebrews] to guard you on the way [to Canaan] and bring you to the place which I have prepared … For My Messenger [the Christ] shall go before you [in the cloud on the Wilderness Journey] and bring you in to the … Canaanites …" Exodus 23:20&23

This luminous cloud went before the Hebrew people as they traveled to Canaan during the day. Then at nightfall it stopped and the people would camp. At night the cloud became fire-like and was called the "pillar of fire." Sometimes, the cloud would come down to a special tent called the "tabernacle." Here Moses would commune with God; would speak to God as a friend; much as Christians do today in "Communion."

When one examines the NT, it is seen that Christ's power over water continued. At Cana in Galilee, Christ turned about 120 gallons of water into wine for a week long wedding feast [John 2:1-10]. Mary, the mother of Jesus, was present at this event and spoke to Jesus about how they had run out of wine for the guests. In the early centuries, before germs were discovered as a cause of disease, wine, with its alcohol content, was a safe drink. It was more than a pleasant diversion; it was a water downed necessity. So, Jesus asked the waiters to fill six stone jars that were present with "two to three firkins" of water. A "firkin" was 20 to 30 gallons. After this task was completed the head waiter was called who then discovered that the water had become wine; probably red wine, the most common kind. And this was then declared to be a better wine than that which had run out!

The third step in this historic sequence was the miraculous happening at the Last Supper. At the Last Supper, Jesus took wine, not unlike that of Cana, and told his apostles that he was changing this wine, which he held in a cup, into his own blood. It would still look like wine, but he assured them, that it was in fact his very own Blood. He then told them to do this same action, as he had just done, when he was gone [Luke 22:19; 1 Cor. 11:24].

In the OT only priests could handle the blood of a sacrificed animal. Likewise, in the NT era, priests of the Church were ordered to consecrate wine into the blood of Christ. He also took some bread in his hands at the Last Supper saying, that it would in a similar way, become his Body. And then after saying these transforming words, held his new Body, in his own hands! This was not some kind of "side show," but was rather meant to speak of his "real presence" under the appearance of Bread and Wine. He would become "personally present," like a father who says that his son is his very own "flesh and blood," present within the family. Each person would be able in the future to "commune" with Christ in the same way Moses had done on the Exodus journey. "Communion" would become the new normal for every Christian at Mass.

12.

New Covenant

After the Hebrews had exited Egypt and been moving slowly through the Wilderness, they came to Mount Sinai.

> "In the third month, when the children of Israel were gone forth out of the land of Egypt … they came into the wilderness of Sinai." Exodus 19:1

At Mt. Sinai, God would descend upon the mountain to speak with Moses. God would give Moses two stone tablets having the Ten Commandments written on them. Then God would ask Moses to present these commandments and other information to the Hebrew people at the foot of the mountain.

> "The Lord said to Moses: 'Come up to me on the mount … and I will give you tablets of stone, and a law and commandments which I

have written; that you may teach them [to the people]." Exodus 24:12

"When I was gone up onto the mount [Mt. Sinai] to receive the tablets of stone, the tablets of the covenant which Yahweh made with you, I stayed on the mountain forty days." Deuteronomy 9:9

On the mountain, Yahweh told Moses that he would be their God if they would make an effort to live by his Commandments. The people agreed to do this and thus an agreement was reached. This agreement is known as a "covenant" and would be sealed by using the "blood" of a sacrificed animal. Moses would sprinkle the blood of the animal upon an altar representing God and then upon the people. The two parties would thereby form an artificial blood kinship bond. They would become in effect one blood, one family.

"Moses rose up early in the morning and built an altar under the hill [of Mt. Sinai] ... And he sent some young men of Israel to offer burnt offerings ... And Moses took half of the blood [of the offered animal] … and sprinkled the altar. He then took the book of the covenant [the Law given to Moses] and read it to an audience of the people; and they said: 'All that Yahweh has said we will do; and [we will] be obedient.' And Moses [then] took the blood and sprinkled it on the people, and said: 'Behold the blood of the covenant [an agreement] which Yahweh has made with you concerning all these words.'" Exodus 24:4-8

These words "blood of the covenant" are the reference point Jesus used at the Last Supper in announcing the Eucharist. St. Paul writes the following, using the words Jesus had given him.

"In the same way also the cup, after [the Passover] supper, [Jesus] saying: 'This cup [of wine] is the new covenant in my Blood. Do this [action] as often as you drink it, in remembrance of me.'" 1 Corinthians 11:25

Luke's report reads in a similar way.

"Likewise, after [the Passover] supper, [Jesus] said: 'This cup [of wine] is the new covenant

in my Blood, which is poured out for you.'"
Luke 22:20

Matthew [26:28] and Mark [14:24] leave out the word "new" as it relates to covenant, both saying: "This is my blood of the covenant, which is poured out for many."

Therefore, Jesus' phrase, "blood of the covenant" mirrors the ancient rite of Exodus 24:4-8, and at the same time points to the new covenant community that his sacrifice has brought into being. The term "new covenant" was first used by the prophet Jeremiah about 600 BC.

> "The days are coming, says Yahweh [God the
> Father], that I will make a new covenant with
> the house of Israel and with the house of Ju-
> dah." Jeremiah 31:31

This statement differs from the "new covenant" of Jesus in at least two ways. First, when Jeremiah wrote this statement the house or kingdom of Israel did not exist as a political entity. It had been conquered in 721 BC by Assyria. Then in 586 BC the kingdom of Judah also became a vassal state. Jerusalem and its Temple were burned to the ground. Thereafter neither Israel or Judah had kings or were kingdoms. The Hebrew people were thereafter controlled by the ruler in Babylon [today's Bagdad].

Second, the future "new covenant" that Jeremiah spoke of was a time-bound agreement. It spoke of earthly kingdoms; whereas the "new covenant" of which Jesus spoke was eternal. It was to last forever. The kingdom of which Jesus spoke was the Kingdom of God [Matt 26:29; Luke 22:30; 1 Corinthians 15:24]. So, while Jesus used the terminology of Jeremiah, he meant a covenant which was fulfilled in Heaven. And the means of getting to Heaven was to receive the Lord in Holy Communion, mankind's "daily bread" [Matt 6:11]; and to live or act upon the Commandments given by God on Mt Sinai [1 John 2:3, 3:24].

Celebration of the Eucharist
Artwork from Memorize the Mass!
(En Route Books and Media, 2016), authored by Kevin Vost,
artist Ted Schluenderfritz

13.

Temple with "Bread of the Presence"

Along with the Ten Commandments, Yahweh gave Moses additional instructions at Mt. Sinai. One of these instructions was for Moses to build an enclosure or "house" for Yahweh. Yahweh intended to be personally present within the Hebrew community, as they moved toward the "promised land" of Canaan [later to be known as "Israel"].

> "Let them make for me a sanctuary; [or house] that I may dwell among them; according to all that I am going to reveal to you [Moses], the plan of the tabernacle." Exodus 25:8-9

> "The tabernacle [or house] of Yahweh ... Moses had made in the Wilderness." 1 Chronicles 21:29

The "tabernacle" was a rectangular "tent" that could be taken down whenever the Hebrews moved over land. It had two small spaces inside, divided by a veil.

In the first room, called the "Holy Place" was a seven branched candle-stand [for light] and a table with the "Bread of the Presence" sitting on it [the literal English of the Hebrew "lehem happanim" is "breads of the Face"]. This "Face" referred to God's face with whom Moses had spoken [Exodus 33:11].

> "Seek Yahweh and his strength; seek his face without ceasing. Remember his wonders that he has done, his miracles and the judgments of his mouth." Psalm 105:45

In the second room, called the "Holy of Holies," the "Ark of the Covenant" resided. It included a 4x2x2 foot wooden box covered inside and out with gold. Inside the box were two tablets with the Ten Commandments etched on them by God. A jar of Manna was also present according to Exodus 16:32-34 and Hebrews 9:4. The top of the box was also said to be the "mercy seat" of God's Presence.

The Showbread, or Bread of the Presence, in the Holy Place consisted of twelve baked cakes made with wheat flour. They were arranged in two rows on a gold plated table that stood in front of the Holy of

Holies. Each Sabbath day the cakes were changed. The sacred breads of the previous week were then eaten by attending priests.

> "Take flour and bake twelve cakes with it ... You shall set them in two rows, six in a row on the pure table [in the tabernacle-tent] before Yahweh ... it shall be <u>bread for a memorial</u> ... an offering to Yahweh. On every Sabbath day he [a priest] shall arrange it before Yahweh continually [as a gift] from the sons of Israel [the Twelve tribes], <u>a never-ending covenant</u>." Leviticus 24:5-8

> "He [Moses] placed the table in the 'Tent of the Meeting,' in the part of the tabernacle outside the veil. And he set the bread on it before Yahweh, as Yahweh had commanded." Exodus 40:22-23

The tabernacle-tent was a sacred place or locus for God's Presence. Ordinary Hebrews did not enter it. When it was set up, the divine Presence in the Cloud hovered over the camp, which during the day lead the Hebrews on their journey, and at night came down and filled the tent with God's glory. Moses would then speak with God "face to face" about problems of the journey [Exodus 33:11].

> "You [Moses] shall [when the tent is completed] make a wooden table ... and overlay it with pure gold ... and ... set upon the table the Bread of Presence before me [Yahweh] always." Exodus 25:23-24 & 30

> "My Presence [in the tent] shall go with you [Moses], and I will give you rest." Exodus 33:14

> "As Moses walked to the [tabernacle] tent all the people usually rose and stood, each one at the door of his [own] tent, and looked at Moses until he had gone into the [tabernacle] tent and ... as Moses went into the tent, the Pillar of the Cloud would come down [like Jesus of John 6:38] and stand at the door of the tent ... And all the people usually rose and bowed [to God], each one at the door of his [own] tent. And Yahweh would [then] speak

to Moses face to face, as a man speaks to his friend." Exodus 33:8-11

After 40 years of journeying the Hebrew people finally reached Canaan, the "everlasting" home of Israel [Genesis 17:8]. Joshua brought them into the Canaanite land which had been offensive to the Lord because of the idol worship of its native population. After an initial struggle with the native residents, Joshua began to make assignments. Again the mobile tabernacle, or "Tent of the Meeting" appears in the Biblical text.

"The sons of Israel were gathered at Shiloh; and they established there the Tent of the Meeting." Joshua 18:1-3

"These are the inheritances which … Joshua [c. 1400 BC] … and the heads of the tribes … of Israel divided for an inheritance … at Shiloh before Yahweh, at the door of the Tent of the Meeting [or tabernacle]. And thus they finished dividing [up] the land." Joshua 19:51

Four hundred years later, King Solomon was still using the tabernacle-tent. (1 Kings 6:1)

> "Solomon and all the congregation [970 BC]
> went to the high place in Gibeon; for there
> was God's Tent of the Meeting [the taber-
> nacle] that Moses, the servant of Yahweh, had
> made in the Wilderness." 2 Chronicles 1:3

Then about 960 BC the tabernacle-tent was replaced by the newly constructed Temple in Jerusalem. In this new Temple the "Bread of the Presence," or the Show-bread, continued to be a featured part of Hebrew worship.

> "Solomon made all the vessels that were for
> the house of God [the Jerusalem Temple] …
> And the table on which the 'Bread of the Pres-
> ence' rested." 2 Chronicles 4:19 [1 Kings 7:48]

Two hundred years after Solomon, the Showbread was still prominently present in the Jerusalem Temple. For example, it is mentioned during the reign of King Hezekiah of Judah in 700 BC.

"They went to Hezekiah the king and said: 'We have cleansed all the house of Yahweh [the Jerusalem Temple] ... the altar of burnt offering ... and the Showbread table, with its utensils." 2 Chronicles 29:18

Lastly, during Roman times, the table of the Showbread is yet again featured as a part of Hebrew worship. This is evident on the Roman monument called the "Arch of Titus" which can still be seen in Rome today. This arch was built by the Romans to remember their victory in Jerusalem. In 70 AD, the Romans burned Jerusalem and its Temple to the ground. On the Arch of Titus, etched into its stone, is a picture of the Showbread table from the Jerusalem Temple. Jesus had told his apostles of this upcoming event forty years before it happened.

"About the buildings of the Temple [in Jerusalem] ... I [Jesus] say to you: 'Not one stone here will be left upon another; all will be thrown down.'" Matthew 24:1-2

But what was to replace Temple worship and its "Bread of the Presence" or the "Showbread" in the

Holy Place? The answer is the Bread of Christ's Presence in the Eucharist. Such an understanding is mirrored in the very words of Christ at the Last Supper. For example, compare the Temple text, "Bread for a memorial" [the Showbread] of Leviticus 24:7 with the words of Christ in Luke 22:19: "… this [Bread] is my Body … the remembrance of me." Also in Leviticus 24:8 the words "never ending covenant" are used. By comparison, Jesus used this word "covenant" only one time in the NT; at the Last Supper where he spoke of the "New Covenant" in association with the Eucharist [Luke 22:20].

Walking into a Catholic Church on this planet one will immediately see an altar, and usually behind the altar there will be a "tabernacle." This tabernacle will consist of a rectangular box about two square feet in size. Inside the tabernacle will be reserved consecrated "hosts" from some previous "Mass" celebration. Such hosts of Christ's Presence, the Eucharist, are usually taken to sick persons either in their homes or in nearby hospitals. These consecrated hosts carry the Lord's personal presence to anyone in need. They carry the Lord's personal outreach to us. They are the visible sign of what Christians call "Holy Communion" with the Lord. They are the visible evidence that the Church is doing what the Lord said it was to do at the Last Supper. That directive was to consecrate bread and wine to become Christ's Body and Blood Presence here on earth. It was a way of extending his incarnation, his walk with us upon this planet.

The Lord, therefore, has provided a long history of the word "tabernacle," even before it appeared inside a church. Notice too that, within the NT, Jesus "tented [or tabernacle-d] among us."

> "In the beginning was the Word, and the Word was with God [the Father], and the Word [Jesus] was God [the Son] … and the Word became flesh [in the fullness of time] and tented among us and we beheld his glory [in his Face]." John 1:1-3 & 14

> "He was transfigured in front of them [Peter, James and John] and his face shown like the sun." Matthew 17:2

14.

Kingdom of God

At the Last Supper, Jesus consecrated bread and wine to be his ongoing Body and Blood Presence on this planet. Since Jesus brought this world into existence from nothing, he certainly has the power to alter bread and wine to become his own ongoing Presence [Hebrews 11:3]. Furthermore, he also possessed the authority to authorize others to do this action in his Name and by his power.

When Jesus finished this transforming action at the Last Supper, technically known as "transubstantiation," he immediately spoke of the "Kingdom of God." Why did he do this? Why was this topic immediately addressed?

> "Jesus took bread ... and said: 'Take, eat; this is my Body.' And [then] he took the cup [of wine] ... saying: ' ... this is my Blood ... But I say to you, I will not drink henceforth ... until

that day when I drink it new with you in my Father's Kingdom.'" Matthew 26:26-29

The text of Mark's account is nearly identical except for its ending: " … until that day that I drink it new in the Kingdom of God." Mark 14:22-25

The text of Luke says that Jesus spoke of the "Kingdom of God" before he consecrated the bread. This could mean that Jesus spoke of the Kingdom of God both before and after his blessing of the bread and wine.

"I will not drink of the fruit of the vine [wine], until the Kingdom of God shall come. And [then] he took bread … saying: 'This is my Body which is given for you: this do [you] in remembrance of me.'" Luke 22:18-19

As a topic, it seems that the Kingdom of God is closely aligned with the Eucharistic mystery. The Eucharist may be the "daily Bread" of which Jesus spoke when he gave humans the "Lord's Prayer" in Matt

6:11. "Your Kingdom come ... Give us today our daily Bread." This nourishment, that gives one real life, meaning "everlasting life," is certainly the Eucharist [John 6:27]. It is what we should mean, when we say that someone is "full of life."

"God [the Father] ... gave [to us] his only be-gotten Son [Jesus], that whoever believes in him should not perish but have everlasting life." John 3:16

"Of his [Jesus'] Kingdom there shall be no end." Luke 1:33

"I [Jesus] say to you: 'There are some standing here who will not taste [their own] death be-fore they see the Son of Man [myself, the risen Lord] coming in his Kingdom.'" Matt 16:28 [Mark 9:1]

This Kingdom of which Jesus spoke is situated be-yond death. His resurrection revealed its certain ex-istence.

"My Kingdom is not of this world." John 18:36

One enters this Kingdom of God, revealed by Jesus, through the sacrament of Baptism.

"Jesus answered … 'unless a man is born [again] of water and of the Spirit [in Baptism], he cannot enter into the Kingdom of God." John 3:15

"Peter said to them: 'Repent [of your sin], and be baptized every one of you." Acts 2:38

"Baptism now saves you." 1 Peter 3:21

"[We] were baptized into Christ Jesus." Romans 6:3

Christians who have been baptized are "in Christ"; and are thereby to live a sacrificial life like that of Christ. "It is no longer I [Paul] who live, but Christ [who] lives in me." Galatians 2:20

"We suffer with him that we may also be glorified together [with him]." Romans 8:17

The problem here is that Christians "in Christ" still fall into sin. So how can this problem of sin be controlled or minimized? The early saints recommended frequent Holy Communion as the best aid for getting into Heaven. Communion, along with the Spirit's help, is a powerful aid directing Christians toward Heaven. And this is probably why Jesus placed the Eucharist next to a discussion of the Kingdom of God during the Last Supper. St Ignatius of Antioch, a bishop who was martyred in Rome in 107 AD, called the Eucharist: " ... the medicine of immortality and the antidote to prevent us from dying [being lost]" [Letter to the Christians at Ephesus 20].

The concept of a "kingdom" and of its "kings" was not unknown to the Hebrew people. Israel had been organized into a kingdom a thousand years before Christ. The story goes something like this. As Israel entered the promised land of Canaan, their King was said to be Yahweh. The land of Canaan was divided by Joshua into twelve parts, a part for each of the twelve tribes of Israel. Each parcel of land was then to be ruled by a "judge," who in today's language would be called a "governor." This arrangement lasted from about 1400 -1050 BC. During that period, two things changed the landscape: [1] The Hebrew people started wandering away from Yahweh; they began to adopt some of the gods of the Canaanites. [2] A second problem also surfaced. The Philistine people, who resided near the Mediterranean coast, became more aggressive toward the Hebrew occupation. These two factors motivated the Hebrew people into seeking a king to rule over them as a unified kingdom. Initially, this idea was opposed by God, but eventually the prophets revealed God's approval. God would let them experiment with an earthly kingdom and a king. This would prepare them for the revelation of the Kingdom of God at a later date.

The first person to become king of Israel was Saul. However, Saul behaved more like a war lord than a king. For example, he did not found a capitol or develop an administration. Eventually, David replaced Saul as the king of Israel. David made Jerusalem his capitol and developed an effective army and administration. He required each of the twelve tribes of Israel to finance the new government for one month a year. David ruled from about 1010 to 972 BC. Then, his son Solomon became king. Solomon set up a system of extreme taxation that alienated his people. As a result of this maltreatment, when Solomon died the Kingdom of Israel was split into two kingdoms: Israel to the north and Judah to the south. Each of these two kingdoms then had a long line of ineffective and sometimes immoral kings. Israel had 18 kings and then was conquered by Assyria in 721 BC. At that time Israel was dissolved as a kingdom and became a vassal state. Judah had 20 kings and then was conquered by Babylonia in 586 BC. Judah also was dissolved as a kingdom. Thereafter, Israel and Judah were controlled by other peoples: first the Persians, then the Greeks, and finally the Romans. From 586 BC until the coming of Christ, Israel was not a kingdom. During that time the Hebrew people began looking for a "Messiah," one who would lead them out of this bondage. They wanted a new king and kingdom which would stand up against the Romans, or others, if necessary.

Jesus surprised many within the Jewish population! They wanted an earthly kingdom, whereas Jesus revealed a heavenly Kingdom. Israel's previous history should have taught them that an earthly kingdom would eventually die out, would not last. However, the Kingdom of God, which Jesus revealed, would last forever. His was an "eternal" Kingdom.

> "The eternal Kingdom of our Lord and deliverer Jesus Christ." 2 Peter 1:11

Within the discussion of "kingdoms" should be a discussion of the more general concept of "the world." While it is known that kingdoms will eventually fail, many people live on earth today as if "the world" will last forever. People of the modern era often use most of their time accumulating wealth in the form of large houses, expensive cars, prestigious employment, and large bank accounts. These items, if not treated properly, that is in a spiritual way, can basically be viewed as "idols." It was with this form of idolatry in mind that Satan presented his last temptation to Christ in the desert.

"Again, the Devil ... showed him [showed Jesus] all the kingdoms of the world and their splendor, and said to him: 'All these I will give you, if you will fall down and worship me.' Then Jesus said to him: 'Go Satan; for it has been written: Worship the Lord your God and serve him only.'" Matthew 4:8-10

The "world" before us is in fact passing away. We should not treat it as an idol.

"What does it benefit a man to gain the whole world but lose his soul ... ?" Matthew 16:26

One should set out instead to attain the following.

"Blessed is he who shall eat bread in the Kingdom of God." Luke 14:15

15.

Temple of His Body

God is present everywhere in the universe. He is the primary cause of all the secondary causes that hold the universe together. The universe itself might be compared to a chandelier suspended on nothing; held there by God.

> "All things were made by him [Christ], and without him not anything was made that was made." John 1:3

> "He [Christ] is before all [things], and all [things] in him hold together." Colossians 1:17

The universe as a whole can be viewed as the "temple" of God. He is present everywhere in it!

What then is the "Temple of Jerusalem" that one reads about in the Bible? The Jerusalem Temple is God's special place of his Presence on this planet for his Chosen People – Israel. God insisted on this place so that the Hebrew people would always know that he was before them. That is why even today thousands of Jews stand by the Western Wall in Jerusalem and pray. The Western Wall is the only portion of the Jerusalem Temple still in existence. The Romans burned the Jerusalem Temple to the ground in 70 AD.

EXODUS TEMPLE

This notion of God's Presence in a temple began at Mt. Sinai about 1406 BC, when God told Moses how to build him a tabernacle-tent, or "house."

> "Moses … raised up its polls. And he spread out the tent-cover over the tabernacle … He [then] brought the Ark [a wooden box containing the Ten Commandments] into the tabernacle … into the Tent of Meeting." Exodus 40:18-22

When Moses had finished the construction of Yahweh's "house," the "Pillar of the Cloud" that hovered over the Hebrew camp, came down from the sky and filled the tabernacle-tent.

"The Cloud covered the Tent of Meeting and the glory of Yahweh [God the Father] filled the tabernacle; so that [even] Moses was not able to go into the Tent." Exodus 40:34-35

The Tabernacle with God's Presence was the central feature in Hebrew life. The Pillar of the Cloud led the people during the day and then at night settled upon the Tabernacle. This pattern lasted forty years until the Hebrew people were allowed to enter the promised land of Canaan [what is today Israel].

"The Tabernacle was set up and the cloud covered it on that day. Then from evening until morning the cloud over the Tabernacle appeared to be a 'pillar of fire' ... When the cloud lifted from the sacred tent, the people of Israel followed it; and whenever the cloud settled [on the tent] the people of Israel camped. In this way they traveled at the Lord's command, and stopped wherever he told them to. They remained where they were as long as the cloud stayed over the Tabernacle." Numbers 9:15-18

Moses would also receive revelation or instructions from God in the Tent of Meeting.

> "As Moses went into the tent the 'pillar of the cloud' [with God present therein] would come down and stand at the door of the tent; and he spoke with Moses." Exodus 33:9

> "I will sanctify the Tabernacle of the congregation and the altar ... And I will dwell in the midst of the sons of Israel ... I am Yahweh their God who brought them out from the land of Egypt that I may dwell in their midst." Exodus 29:44-46

TEMPLE IN CANAAN

The Hebrew people lived with Yahweh forty years in the Wilderness before entering Canaan. Once they entered Canaan, what would eventually be called "Israel," they set up the Tabernacle-tent in various places.

"In Shiloh, before Yahweh at the door of the Tent of Meeting, they finished dividing up the land." Joshua 19:51

"For the Tabernacle of Yahweh, which Moses made in the Wilderness, and the altar of the burnt offering, were at that season in … Gibeon." 1 Chronicles 21:29

SOLOMON'S TEMPLE

During the reign of King David [1010-972 BC] God indicated to the prophet Nathan that he wanted a more permanent "house" for his Presence.

"Thus says Yahweh: 'Will you build a [more permanent] house for me … I have dwelt in a [tent] house since the day I brought the sons of Israel up from Egypt … I've been moving about in a tent." 2 Samuel 7:5-6

King Solomon, David's son, completed the building of the Temple in Jerusalem about 960 BC. When Solomon dedicated the Temple building, the luminous

Cloud of Yahweh's Presence from the Exodus period, filled the house.

> "The priests brought the Ark of the Covenant of Yahweh (God the Father) to its place [in the Temple] … into the Holy of Holies … And it was then, when the priests went out … that the Cloud filled the house of Yahweh; and the priests were not able to stand up to minister … for the glory of Yahweh had filled the house [or Temple] of Yahweh." 1 Kings 8:6-11

ISAIAH IN THE TEMPLE

Two hundred years later, in the year 739 BC the prophet Isaiah experienced a similar occurrence. He saw Yahweh sitting on a throne high up in the Jerusalem Temple. The entire Temple was filled with smoke, resembling the fiery Cloud containing Yahweh's Presence during the nighttime hours on the Exodus.

> "In the year [when] King Uzziah died, I saw Yahweh sitting on a high throne, and the train of his robe filled the Temple. Angels stood above him … And one cried to another, and

said: 'Holy, holy, holy is Yahweh of hosts. All the earth is filled with his glory.' And the posts of the threshold shook from the voices, and the house was filled with smoke." Isaiah 6:1-4

NEW TEMPLE IN 516 BC

The Jerusalem Temple that was built under the direction of King Solomon remained the focus of God's Presence for about 400 years. Then in 586 BC, it was burnt to the ground by the Babylonians under Nebuchadnezzar. Many thousands of Jerusalem residents were taken to Babylon as prisoners and not released until 538 BC when a new king came to power. After the Hebrews returned from exile, they built a new Temple in Jerusalem, completed in 516 BC. The prophet Ezekiel was present for its dedication and described the return of Yahweh to this New Temple. Once again the Cloud of Yahweh's Presence was there.

"The glory of Yahweh came [again] into the Temple through the east gateway." Ezekiel 43:4

"Then the man brought me through the north gateway to the front of the Temple. I looked and saw that the glory of Yahweh [the illuminated cloud] filled the Temple of Yahweh. And I fell [to the floor] on my face." Ezekiel 44:4

"I [Yahweh] will put my sanctuary in their midst forever." Ezekiel 37:26

In this new Temple, Israel worshipped God from 516 BC until about 70 AD. In 70 AD the Roman army destroyed this Second Temple in Jerusalem. Only the Western Wall of that Temple remains today. It was not rebuilt. At the same time "animal sacrifice" as it had been done in the Jerusalem Temple and elsewhere, also came to an end. It was replaced by the study of the Torah and by "personal sacrifice," meaning the sacrifices made within a human life to help others, to improve oneself, or to improve the world.

"Present your bodies as a living sacrifice, holy and well pleasing to God, the reasonable service." Romans 12:1

TEMPLE OF CHRIST'S BODY

From Abraham, through Moses and King David, and the prophets, God had promised that he would be forever present to his chosen people. He also promised further that his personal Presence would eventually reach out to everyone on earth so as to guide and comfort them on their journey to Heaven. To meet this new need, God reached back into the Exodus, to the bread-like "Manna," which he had given the Hebrew people on their journey to the promised land of Canaan. God would again use bread, this time empowering it to carry his very Presence. This new bread, the "Eucharist," would not just empower the bodies of people, as it had done during the Wilderness Journey; it would give them eternal life if they made it a part of themselves. In a mysterious way, the Lord's Presence in the Eucharist would lead them to Heaven. It would offer them the Lord's Presence on their arduous journey back to the Father.

The first six chapters of the Gospel of John offer some penetrating insights as to how the Temple of Christ would became established on this planet. This Temple established by Christ was not made by human hands.

Chapter 1 of John opens with Jesus, the Father's Word, becoming "flesh" and tenting [or tabernacle-ing] among the peoples of earth.

> "In the beginning [of the universe] was the Word, and the Word was with God [the Father], and the Word was God [the Son, Jesus] … And the Word [in the fullness of time] became flesh [at Bethlehem] and tented [or tabernacled] among us and we beheld his glory [as in the luminous cloud of the Exodus or within the Jerusalem Temple]." John 1:1-3;14

Chapter 2 of John reports how Jesus removed from the Temple those who sold animals for sacrifice or changed differing kinds of money. These activities should have been located on the streets outside the Temple buildings. Jesus said that God's house should be used only as a house of prayer. The Jews in charge of the Temple complex asked him to work a miracle or "sign" to prove his authority to say and do such things. Jesus said to them that if God's Temple was destroyed, he could raise it in three days. Their response implied that he was a little crazy to make such a claim.

> "The Jews said: 'It took 46 years to build [meaning to repair] this Temple [in Jerusalem]; and you [Jesus] will raise it in 3 days?!'" But he [the Christ] spoke about the Temple of his [own] body." John 2:20-21

What Jesus was saying here was that his body is the true Temple – the universal Temple.

He is the only divine Person ever to be "seen" on this planet [John 1:18]. To raise his body from the dead would take three days as stated. Once raised [on Easter] his body would be seen as "glorified," not unlike the luminous Presence of God in the Cloud on the Exodus or in the Temple of Ezekiel's time.

In the phrase "Temple of his body," there were two possible Greek words that could have been used for the word "Temple." One of these words described the whole Temple complex with its several structures. The other word, used here, referred only to the inner sanctuary where the divine Cloud stayed. This implies that Jesus' body is that inner sanctuary of the Jerusalem Temple, the "Holy of Holies."

Chapter 4 of John speaks of a conversation between Jesus and a Samaritan woman. In this conversation, Jesus makes the following statement.

> "Believe me, woman, an hour is coming when neither on this mountain [in Samaria] nor in Jerusalem [where the Temple is] will you worship the Father. You worship what you know not; we [in Jerusalem] worship what we know, because salvation [meaning the coming of Christ] is from the Jews." John 4:21-22

What Christ says here is that he is God. He is the one to be worshipped. His body is the New Temple, wherever it is located.

Chapter 5 of John answers the question of how "the world" can find Jesus.

> "You [OT people] search the scriptures because you think that in them you have eternal life; but they are [really] those that [give] witness to me [the Christ]." John 5:39

This theme is found in many places in the NT. Notice these examples.

"Beginning from Moses [1406 BC] and from all the prophets [1406-150 BC] he [the risen Christ] explained to them in the [OT] scriptures the things concerning himself." Luke 24:27

"We have found [the Christ] of whom Moses in the law and [the OT] prophets wrote." John 1:4

"To him (Christ) all the prophets give witness." Acts 10:43

Chapter 6 of John explains more about this New Temple, who is Christ. The materials of this New Temple will be the bread and wine of common use, which will be transformed or transfigured into the Body and Blood of Christ. This will be done by the divine Word through an exercise of Christ's own power.

"The bread of [eternal] life is the one coming down out of Heaven [like the shiny Cloud of

the Exodus] … I [Christ] am the Bread of
[eternal] life." John 6:33-34; 41

"I [Christ] am the living Bread, the one having come down out of Heaven. If anyone eats
of this [transformed] Bread he will live to the
age [forever]." John 6:51

This notion of "living Bread," or Bread that is alive,"
meaning the Person of Christ, was also very much on
the mind of St Paul.

"We are the temple of the living God; as God
said: 'I will house [myself] IN them and I will
be for them God and [they] will be my [new
covenant] people." 2 Cor 6:16

The container, or the person carrying God's Eucha-
ristic Presence, would be the outer part of this New
Temple. The inner part of the Temple, the "Holy of
Holies," is the Lord Jesus himself.

JERUSALEM TEMPLE IS DESTROYED

The Gospel of Matthew presents several passages that outline the Jerusalem Temple in its last days. There are at least six steps in this transition from the OT Temple to the NT Temple.

First. In chapter 12 of Matthew, Jesus addressed the issue of who can or cannot eat the sacred bread within the Temple. The answer had always been: "only the priests of the Temple can eat the bread." However, Jesus pointed out that, when King David and his men were hungry, they entered the Temple and ate the sacred bread. By saying this, Jesus was pointing to the future, when his followers would enter a church building and receive the Eucharist.

> "David, when he and his companions hungered … entered the house of God [the Jerusalem Temple] and ate the Bread of the Presence, which it was not lawful for him or his companions to eat; but [was] only [to be eaten by] the priests." Matthew 12:3-4

Then Jesus made the following eye opening statement, speaking of himself. "I [Jesus] say to you: a greater is here than the [Jerusalem] Temple." Mt 12:6. Jesus was speaking of himself!

Second. In chapter 17 of Matthew, the "Transfiguration" of Jesus is narrated. In this event, Jesus became luminous, like God in the burning bush [Exodus 3:2], or God within the shiny Cloud of the sacred-tent on the Wilderness Journey [Exodus 13:21]. In the Transfiguration one sees the "Shekinah glory" of God. The Transfiguration shows Christ's "metamorphosis" from one body form [earthly] into another body form [risen].

This event is reported in four places in the NT: Matt 17:1-9; Mark 9:1-13; Luke 9:28-36; and 2 Peter 1:16-18.

"Jesus took Peter. James and John to a high hill ... And he was transformed in front of them; and his face was shown as the sun, and his clothes became white as light [not unlike the burning bush of Moses' experience]. And behold Moses [1450 BC] and Elijah [850 BC] were seen by them [the Apostles] speaking with him [Jesus]. And Peter said … 'I will make three tents here [as on the Exodus] for you …' While he was still speaking a bright Cloud [as on the Exodus] overshadowed them; and a voice [God the Father] out of the Cloud said: 'This [Jesus] is my Son … hear him.'" Mt 17:1-5

Third. In chapter 23 of Matthew, Christ spoke of exiting the Jerusalem Temple permanently. During his public life he had regularly entered and left the Temple, each time doing the Father's instructional work.

"By day I [Jesus] sat in the Temple teaching, and you did not hold me [back]." Mt 26:55

Now Jesus speaks of leaving the Temple for good. This exiting of Jesus from the Temple resembled God's departure before the destruction of Solomon's Temple in 586 BC. The prophet Ezekiel spoke of how the cloud-like Presence of God exited the Temple in his day [Ezekiel 8:5-6; 9:3]. Now Jesus explains why he is leaving the Temple during his time.

"I [Jesus] wished to gather your [Jewish] children; as a bird gathers her young under her wings, but you [parents] wished not. Look, your house [the Temple] is left to you desolate." Mt 23:37-38

Fourth. In chapter 24 of Matthew, Jesus became more specific about the future of the Jerusalem Temple. Speaking about 30 AD, he said that the Jerusalem Temple would be destroyed. This occurred in 70 AD when the Roman army, led by the future emperor Titus, burned the Temple to the ground. It was never rebuilt. There would be no new man-made Temple. The New Temple had already become the Body of Christ. Scripture speaks of this.

"Christ ... the greater and more complete tent (temple), not handmade and not of this creation." Hebrews 9:11

"[Christ] spoke about the Temple of his own Body." John 2:21

"The disciples approached [Christ] to show him the (great) buildings of the [Jerusalem]

> Temple. And he … said to them … 'by no
> means will there be left here stone on stone,
> which shall not be overthrown.'" Mt 24:1-2

Jesus however was wrong! The Western Wall, or "Wailing Wall," a portion of the Temple, is still standing. This is therefore a subtle indication that Jesus' statement about the Temple's demise was recorded before the Temple was actually destroyed by the Romans. The remark, therefore, implies the work of early writers.

Fifth. In chapter 27 of Matthew, the reader learns of Jesus' death. At that moment, the heavy curtain that separated the inner from the outer part of the Jerusalem Temple was torn in two pieces from the top to the bottom [probably due to the earthquake of Mt 27:51]. This top-down tearing symbolized the end of the Temple. It also opened up the "Holy of Holies," the inner most part of the Temple, to everyone. It was here that God's special Presence resided; and where only the high priest had been earlier able to enter once a year for the people. Jesus had already spoken of his own Body as the new Temple, or "Holy of the Holies," as reported in John 2:21.

"[Christ] spoke about the Temple [literally the, 'Holy of Holies'] of his [own] Body." John 2:21

His Body, following the Last Supper bread and wine instructions, would eventually be available to everyone!

"Jesus ... released his spirit [on the cross] and behold the veil of the Temple was rent [torn] in two from above to below." Matthew 27:51 [Mark 15:38; Luke 23:45]

Sixth. Lastly, in chapter 28 of Matthew, it is revealed that Christ, who is the New Temple for all peoples on earth, will be forever among us.

"Where two or three are assembled in my name, there I am [or will be] in the midst of them ... Behold I am with you all days until the completion of the age." Mt 18:20 & 28:20

CHRIST'S "MYSTICAL BODY" AS TEMPLE

In the OT God's special Presence was to be among his people. He was in the midst of them as they moved about. In the NT era God would come even closer. God would reside inside his people. The Spirit would enliven them; and the Lord Jesus would live within them by his special Presence, the Eucharist.

This special Presence of the Lord Jesus is singular. Consecrated bread is always one Body. It is not space or time bound. On any Sunday morning, Mass is celebrated all over the planet and in differing time zones. It is still one Body, though simultaneously present in many places. The Mystical Body of Christ is a new form of God's Temple. The Person of Christ and the Spirit are at its center [the "Holy of Holies"], and we, the members of Christ's Body, are its outer structure [the "Holy Place"]. St. Paul describes this new Temple in various ways, especially using as a model the human body with its many members.

> "The bread which we break is it not a communion of the Body of Christ? Because [we receive] one Bread, we the many are one

[Mystical] Body; for we all partake of the one Bread." 1 Cor 10:16-17

"You are ... members of the household of God, having been built on the foundation of the [OT} prophets and [NT] apostles; Christ himself being the cornerstone, in whom all the building is joined together, growing into a holy Temple in the Lord." Eph 2:19-21

"There is one [Mystical] Body [of Christ] and one Spirit [in the Body] ... one faith, one baptism, one God and Father of all ..." Eph 4:4-6

"We the many are one [Mystical] Body in Christ and each one members of another." Rom 12:5

"The Church, which is his [Christ's] Body, the fullness of the [one] filling all things." Eph 1:23

Christ is the "cornerstone" because as St. Paul says in 1 Corinthians 15:22: "In Christ all will be made alive" [with eternal life]. In 1 Peter 2:5 Christians are said to be as "living stones," not unlike "members" in the Body of Christ.

> "Yourselves as living stones are being built [into] a spiritual house [or Temple] … [to offer] spiritual sacrifices acceptable to God [the Father] through Jesus Christ." 1 Peter 2:5

THE TEMPLE IN HEAVEN

In Heaven, there are no Temple buildings. In Heaven, the Temple is God the Father and his Word, the "Lamb of God," Jesus. This one God is the "Holy of Holies" of the heavenly Temple. This is a Temple "not made with human hands."

> "I will destroy this Temple [in Jerusalem] that is made with hands, and in three days I [Jesus] will build another [namely my risen Body], not made with hands." Mark 14:58

In Heaven, the outer portion of the Temple consists of ordinary people, saints, wherein the Holy Spirit resides. These are the ones who overcame the temptations of the world and who followed Jesus. In Heaven, the saints make up that portion of the Temple formerly known as the "Holy Place."

> "The one conquering [sin 21:7-8] I [Jesus] will make him a pillar [or column] in the Temple of God." Rev 3:12

> "They [in Heaven] are before the throne of God, and serve him day and night in his Temple. And the one sitting on the throne will tent [or tabernacle] among them. They will hunger no more, and thirst no more ... and God will wipe away all tears from their eyes ..." Rev 7:15-17

The heavenly Temple looks back in time to the "tent" of the Exodus. There, God gave the Hebrew people Manna to eat in the desert [bread to satisfy their hunger] and water from the Rock [to satisfy their thirst]. Jesus later promised, in his public life, to permanently satisfy these needs. In Heaven, these needs are forever met.

> "Jesus said to them: 'I am the bread of life; he that comes to me shall never hunger; and he

that believes in me shall never thirst.'" John 6:35

"The Temple of God was opened in Heaven and the Ark of the Covenant was seen in his Temple; and lightning and thunder and shaking occurred [as on Mt. Sinai during the Exodus]." Rev 11:19

The Ark of the Covenant was the 4x2x2 foot box with a stone copy of the Ten Commandments inside. The point is that the covenant is still in effect in Heaven. The Commandments are to be followed in Heaven, and God will keep his covenant promises forever. Heaven will therefore be a Heavenly place.

"Was opened the Temple of the testimony in Heaven ... And the Temple was filled with smoke of the glory of God and of his power ..." Rev 15:5 & 8

The phrase "smoke of the glory of God" refers back to the Presence of God in the tent [or tabernacle] on the Exodus; or to the "Shekinah glory" in the OT Temple. The main point here is that God is fully Present in

Heaven as he had earlier been Present in his Temple on earth.

16.

A Pure Sacrifice

Toward the time of Christ, the sacrificial system of the OT was in decline. The "synagogue" approach to worship was beginning to take hold. This method of worship probably originated in Babylon when the people of Israel were without their Temple. The Temple in Jerusalem had been destroyed in 586 BC by Nebuchadnezzar of Babylon.

Large numbers of Hebrew speaking people were taken to Babylon as prisoners. They were held there until a new king freed them about fifty years later, and it was not until 516 BC that a new Temple in Jerusalem was completed. During this time, in Babylon, the Hebrew people had to rely on the OT scriptures and on prayer for worship. There was no Temple for the offering of animal sacrifices. Later, in Jerusalem, the Temple sacrifices and the synagogue method of worship would exist side by side. However, deficiencies began to appear in the system of worship based upon animal sacrifice. The priests became lax in the kind of animals they used upon the altar. Sheep, goats, and cattle were sometimes blind, lame or diseased – not appropriate as offerings for the good God [Malachi 1:7-8]. And general loyalty regarding other Covenant promises became a problem, especially promises involving marriage [Malachi 2:14-16]. These and other laxities were discussed in one of the late prophetic books: the Book of Malachi.

Malachi was probably written between 460-430 BC. It speaks especially of the failure of OT priests to fear the Lord. It goes on to say that the people followed their example with an indifference toward the will of God. Malachi then attempts to turn the Hebrew people away from their spiritual apathy and to correct priests in their methods of doing worship. The prophesy further speaks of honoring the Lord with "a pure food offering," probably meaning a type of bloodless sacrifice. It also speaks of a day when the Lord will purge and refine his people. For example, Malachi 3:1-6 speaks of a "messenger of the covenant" to do this work of purifying.

Christians later see the work of Christ as this "pure offering" spoken of in Malachi 1:11. Christ is the "blameless" one from God the Father, bringing a "pure" sacrifice and a "New Covenant," for all people on earth.

> "[OT] priests who despise my name ... You are offering defiled food on my altar ... If you present the blind [animal] for sacrifice is it not evil? And if you present the lame and the sick [animal] is it not evil? Present it [a lame or sick animal] to your [Persian] governor! Will he accept it? says the Lord of hosts." Malachi 1:6-8

> "From the rising of the sun to its going down [i.e., throughout the world] my name shall be in every place among the [non-Jewish] nations. And incense shall be offered in my name, and a <u>pure food offering</u> ... says Yahweh of hosts." Malachi 1:11

> "The Lord [Jesus] ... shall suddenly come to his Temple, the messenger of the covenant ... says Yahweh of hosts. But who can endure the day of his coming? ... he is like a refiner's fire." Malachi 3:1-2 [John 2:15]

The words "a pure food offering … offered in my name" is seen by Catholic Christians as referring to the Eucharist. It could not, for example, refer to pure sacrifices being offered to Yahweh throughout the world because that had never happened, nor could it happen. In fact, burnt offerings, whether of animals or of plants, was discontinued after the Jerusalem Temple was burned to the ground in 70 AD. From 70 AD forward, Jewish worship has centered solely upon the Synagogue with its study of OT scriptures, especially of the "law of Moses," the Torah.

The word "pure" in the phrase "pure offering" adds yet another level of meaning. It suggests a perfect offering, which certainly points to Christ.

> "Christ who … offered himself, blameless to God [the Father], [now] cleans our conscience [freeing us] from dead works to serve the living God." Hebrews 9:14

> "Christ … a blameless lamb without stain [of sin]" 1 Peter 1:19

The early Church fathers recognized this connection between the "pure offering" of Malachi 1:11 and the Eucharist of Christian worship. Probably the earliest Christian document to speak of Malachi 1:11 in this way was the "Didache" [Greek for "Teaching"]. This document may date to about 35 AD because of the early form of its prayer used over the bread and wine of the Eucharist.

> "We thank you, our Father, for the holy vine of David [illustrating the early attachment to Judaism] … which you made known to us through Jesus your servant." Didache 9, 2

> "On us you have bestowed a spiritual food and drink (consecrated bread and wine) that lead to eternal life, through Jesus …" Didache 10, 3

Chapter 14 of the Didache used the words of Malachi 1:11 within its text.

> "Every Lord's day [Sunday] gather yourselves together and break bread [the Eucharist, Acts 2:42], and give thanks after having confessed

your sins [John 20:23] that your sacrifice may
be pure. But let no one who is at odds with his
fellow [man] come together with you until
they be reconciled, that your sacrifice may not
be profaned, for this is that which was spoken
by the Lord: 'In every place and time offer to
me a pure sacrifice ..." Didache 14

Another early Church father who refers to Malachi
1:11 was St Justin Martyr [100-165 AD]. A pagan by
birth, Justin studied philosophy before becoming a
Christian in 132 AD. He wrote two "Apologies" addressed to Roman emperors in defense of the Christian faith. Justin quoted the Book of Malachi saying
that its prophesy foretold the age of the Church, when
a "pure sacrifice" would be offered continually and
everywhere on earth.

What follows is a quotation from Justin's *Dialogue
with Trypho*.

"God speaks by the mouth of Malachi ... For
from the rising of the sun to its setting my
name is great among the nations , and in
every place incense is offered to my name,

and a pure offering ... everywhere [in 155 AD] we offer him sacrifice – that is, the bread of the Eucharist and the cup of the Eucharist –affirming that we [non-Jews] glorify his Name." *Dialogue With Trypho* 41

A third early Church father, who viewed the prophesy of Malachi as a signal of the Eucharistic age, was Irenaeus, bishop of Lyons in Gaul [modern France]. Irenaeus was born in Smyrna [Ismir in modern Turkey]. He was a student of Bishop Polycarp [d. 156], who as a young man had known the Apostle John. Irenaeus lived between 140 and 202 AD. His book, *Against Heresies*, was written in opposition to Gnosticism.

"[Jesus] ... took a created thing, bread, and gave thanks, and said: 'This is my Body' [Mt 26:26]. And likewise, the cup [of wine] which is part of the creation to which we belong, he confessed it to be his Blood ... Since the name of the Son [Jesus] belongs to [God] the Father, and since ... the Church makes offerings through Jesus Christ [the divine Person not bound in either space or time] he [Malachi] says rightly: 'And in every place incense is offered to my name, and [also] a pure offering' [Malachi 1:11] … The Lord [also] gave instructions that it [this pure offering] should be offered throughout the world." *Against Heresies* 4.17.5f

"The Temptation of Christ"
Juan de Flandes (c. 1500)
Courtesy of Wikipedia

17.

Stone into Bread

Jesus was a divine Person with a human nature. That is the mystery of the Incarnation. The Devil, or Satan, set out to probe this human dimension of Jesus, to see if Jesus was truly the "Son of God" [Matthew 4:4]. This incident is known as the "Temptation of Jesus" in the desert.

Jesus had been fasting for forty days and nights, so Satan had a great advantage when it came to speaking of "bread." Jesus was hungry! So Satan asked Jesus to change certain desert stones into bread. Jesus refused to do this for Satan, but at the Last Supper he did in fact change bread into his own Body, the Eucharist, his divine Presence – for his followers.

"The one pressuring [meaning Satan] said to him: 'If you are the Son of God, say that these stones might become breads [loaves of bread].' But he [Jesus] answered: 'It has been written [in the OT, Deuteronomy 8:3] that

man shall not live on bread alone, but [rather]
on every word that comes from the mouth of
God.'" Matthew 4:3-4

In these two verses of scripture, the structure of the
Mass and of life itself is laid out.

First, mankind needs the word of God to properly
"inform" himself about ultimate realities and then to
do his life on this planet. In the Mass, this becomes
the "liturgy of the Word": consisting of the OT and
NT readings and the sermon. Second, mankind
needs the "bread of life" to live both on this earth in a
body and spiritually as a divine help in moving us onward toward Heaven. On earth, "bread" empowers
the human body to both work and play. The Eucharist, on the other hand, is "sacred Bread." It empowers
the heart of humans to follow Jesus on his journey
into Heaven. The "liturgy of the Eucharist" is the second half of the Mass. It is the part of Mass where one
"communes" with the Lord concerning particular
problems one has on his or her journey into the
Promised Land of Heaven.

The stones here spoken of were probably the size of a small loaf of unsliced bread: approximately 8x4 inches each. This kind of loaf was probably like the loaf held by Jesus in his hands, at the Last Supper, when he said: "This is my Body."

The apostles would then have taken pieces out of this loaf, after it had become the Body of Christ, each piece also being the Body of Christ. "Sliced bread," as we know it today, was invented about 1920 to fit into the newly invented "toaster." The bread that Jesus used at the Last Supper looked more like the stones found on the desert floor around Jerusalem.

18.

Eucharist in Nature

Bishop Fulton J. Sheen spoke of a "Law of Transformation" within nature. He explained how God has included the Eucharist in the processes of nature. He said that God created chemicals to be transformed into plants, plants into animals, animals into man, and man into the reality of Christ. By this he meant that those who have received the Eucharist have the life of Christ within them.

> "I [St. Paul] live; yet not I, but Christ lives in me
> ..." Galatians 2:20

In other words, Bishop Sheen said that if plants could speak, they would say to animals: "Unless you eat me, you will have no life within you." And if plants and animals could speak, they would say to humans: "Unless you eat me, you will have no life within you." And finally, Christ says to all persons, especially those at Mass:

"Unless you eat Me, during Communion, you will not have My Flesh and Blood Presence within you" meaning that without Christ within, a person will not possess the eternal life of Heaven that Christ promised (John 6:54).

"Reality" is what God makes things to be by his own intention. God's Word is powerful!

> "[Jesus] being the radiance of his [the Father's] glory .... upholding all things by the Word of his power ..." Hebrews 1:3

God's Word brings things into being, into existence. By comparison, man's word is primarily descriptive in nature; people use words to "describe reality," that already exists. The true reality of a thing is what God intends it to be. At the Last Supper Jesus said that consecrated bread would be his Body. He said that at Mass priests were to "do this;" meaning that the deepest reality of bread and wine would be changed by His Words, into His Body and Blood Person. The bread at Mass would look like bread, but because of His intension, it would become in reality his Body. The wine would look like wine, but because of His powerful intention, it would become in fact His Blood. The reality of His Word, together with the action of the priest, will bring the Eucharist into being at Mass. The Eucharist is God's "deep down" intention; becoming the truest reality of the bread and wine within the Mass. The Eucharist becomes at Mass, by His Will, the "Bread of Life," his very "Flesh and Blood" Presence before the people (John 6:35).

"Christ at Emmaus"
Rembrandt (1648)
Courtesy of Wikipedia

19.

Mass on the First Easter

Emmaus is a little town about seven miles from Jerusalem. Emmaus was mentioned in the OT scriptures:1 Maccabees 3:40 and 4:3. Its exact location has recently been discovered. The account of two men walking toward Emmaus, who met and talked with the risen Jesus, is given in Luke 24:13-35.

These two men were "looking sad" when they met Jesus. One of the two men was named "Cleopas." They were speaking with each other about recent events in Jerusalem concerning "Jesus of Nazareth," how the chief priests and rulers had brought about his death. They commented further that they had hoped that Jesus would be the one to "redeem Israel."

These two men, who were disciples of Jesus, did not recognize Jesus as they walked along, because "their eyes were kept from recognizing him" [v. 16]. However, Mark offered a second explanation. Mark said that Jesus "appeared in another form - to the two of them" [Mark 16:12]. Perhaps a resurrection body. This explanation seems very much like a description of the Eucharist itself; that is, being something different from what it appears to be!

The men went on further, saying that something strange had happened. They said that some women in Jerusalem claimed to have seen a "vision of angels," which told them that Jesus of Nazareth was alive – even after being three days in a tomb! And when this claim was investigated by others, they "found it just as the women had said" [v. 24].

At this point Jesus began speaking with the two men. He said that the two of them had been "slow of heart to believe all that the [OT] prophets had spoken of" about Jesus [v. 26]. And he alluded further to the "servant" passage in Isaiah 53:5, asking the question: "Was it not necessary that the Christ should suffer these things and [then] enter into his glory?"

Then, Jesus began, what can be described as the "first Mass" after his resurrection. He began with the "liturgy of the Word." Scripture says that: "Beginning with Moses [books 1-5 of the Bible] and all the [later] prophets, he interpreted for them in all the OT scriptures the things concerning himself" [v. 27]. In other words, Jesus used OT scripture as an introduction to NT revelation. Furthermore, Jesus showed them that his biography was clearly revealed in the OT before his "birth" at Bethlehem. Among the world's population, Jesus is therefore the only person whose biography was known before he was born—an indication of his deity.

Then, Jesus began the second half of Mass, the liturgy of the Eucharist. When the threesome reached Emmaus, Jesus was invited to stay overnight by the other two men. There were few lodging places in those days for overnight guests. Finally, when the threesome sat down to eat, Jesus repeated the actions he had created for the Church at the Last Supper. He [1] took bread, [2] blessed it with his power, [3] broke it into pieces, and [4] gave it to each of the two travelers. At that moment, and only at that moment, did they recognize who Jesus was. Their eyes were opened! And then scripture says: " … he vanished from their sight" [v. 32]. Why did Jesus vanish? Because he had by then become Present in the Eucharistic Bread which he had given to them.

Then the two men got up "in that same hour" and went back to Jerusalem to find the Apostles and tell them what had happened. When they found them, the Apostles had already known that Jesus was risen, and "had [even] appeared to Simon [Peter]" [v. 34]. The two men then proceeded to tell the Apostles what had happened: [1] on the road to Emmaus when the Word was given; and [2] "how Jesus was known to them [only] in the breaking of the Bread [the Eucharist]" [v. 35]. Thus there was a complete Mass: consisting of the liturgy of the Word [with OT Scripture], and the liturgy of the Eucharist [with the action of the Last Supper].

20.

Hidden Manna

During the Exodus from Egypt the Hebrew people were miraculously fed Manna from Heaven. They were given the bread-like Manna during a forty-year period by God. This food sustained the people in their Wilderness Journey to the promised land of Canaan [the future land of Israel].

However, in the NT era, Jesus said that the Manna of the Exodus was not the genuine bread from Heaven because all those who had eaten it had also died. The genuine or true bread from Heaven, he said, is the bread that preserves a person from death. Jesus said further that he alone was that true bread of everlasting life come down from Heaven [John 6:35 & 49-51]. Jesus went on further to say that his own Body is that Bread of everlasting life [John 6:53-58].

Later, at the Last Supper, Jesus would give mankind a palpable form of his "flesh and blood" Presence in the form of the Eucharist. He said that the consecrated

Bread would be his Body and that consecrated Wine would be his life-giving Blood. He himself would thereafter be "hidden" under the appearances of consecrated Bread and Wine.

> "To the one conquering I [God the Father] will give to him the Manna, the one having been hidden [namely Jesus on earth]." Revelation 2:17 [literal English from the NT Greek]

> "You are a God who hides himself [on earth]." Isaiah 45:15

In Heaven, God is not hidden. Those in Heaven see God "face to face."

> "I will seek your face, O Yahweh." Psalm 27:8

> "We look now through a mirror dimly [at Jesus], but then face to face." 1 Corinthians 13:12

In Heaven, the ones "conquering" are eternally in communion with God. These words are therefore directed to the people on earth. By giving people on earth this "hidden Manna," Jesus is giving us himself.

At the Last Supper, Jesus also spoke of a great banquet in the Kingdom of God.

> "I [Jesus] say to you: 'I will not eat of it [the bread] until it is fulfilled in the Kingdom of God … I [also] will not drink of the fruit of the vine [the wine] until the Kingdom of God shall come.'" Luke 22:16 & 18

Luke then provides a summary statement of Jesus's intent.

> "That you may eat and drink at my table in my Kingdom." Luke 22:30

And this Heavenly Banquet is to include all of God's people on this planet.

> "I [Jesus] say to you that many will come from east and west and they will recline [at my table] with Abraham and Isaac and Jacob in the Kingdom of Heaven." Matthew 8:11

Luke then records a parable of Jesus illustrating how careless and sinful those who have been invited to this eternal Banquet can be. The parable is known as "The Parable of the Great Supper" [Luke 14:15-24]. This parable, or little story, begins with the following words of Jesus.

"Blessed is anyone who will eat bread [with me] in the Kingdom of God." Luke 14:15

"A certain man [who was God] made a great dinner, and called everyone [to it] … And they all began to reject [his offer]. The first said: 'I bought a [farm] field and. … have to see it' … The second said: 'I bought five oxen and must approve them' … And a third said: 'I married a woman … and am unable to come' … So the master told his servant: '… go quickly into the wide open places and the lanes of the city and <u>lead</u> the disabled, the blind, and the lame here' … And the servant [after doing this] said: 'There is still room!' So the master said: 'Go out and … <u>compel</u> them to come in, that my house might be full. For I say to you that no one of those having been called [who would not come] will taste of my dinner." Luke 14:15-24

21.

One Flesh Union

Marriage is the union of two human beings: one male and the other female. This union is so profound that it can result in new life being generated within the love of the two persons. This is a sign of the Trinity: Father, Son – and Spirit [the love, the baby].

The primary evidence for the existence of this "love" is the need of the two persons to be together. This need is so dominant that even when apart each person will continually be thinking of the other. A specific marriage begins with the "sighting" of the two persons and then progresses onward toward the "one flesh union" of the marriage relationship.

> "A man [the husband] will leave his father and mother [the source of his flesh] and will be joined to his woman [his wife] and the two will be into one flesh." Ephesians 5:31 [literal English from the NT Greek]

"Men should love their women as their own
bodies [a one flesh union]. The one loving his
woman loves himself [a one flesh union]. No
one ever hates his own flesh, but nourishes
and cherishes it." Ephesians 5:28-29

St. Paul then says in Ephesians 5:32 that this love relationship between a man and a woman is a great
mystery, especially when compared with the relationship between Christ [the groom] and his bride [the
Church]. Paul is here hinting at the "one flesh union"
of Christ with members of his Church. The Eucharist
makes this "one flesh union" possible. The consecrated Bread of Mass, becomes by Christ's promise
and power, his very Flesh or Bodily Presence. The
Body of Christ is then received by "communicants"
into themselves at Mass, thus completing the "one
flesh union" of Christ with each believer. Christ and
his Church are therefore one Body, not unlike the relationship between a husband and wife.

The Incarnation itself is a love story. We are told, by
scripture, that Jesus came to earth as a "groom" looking for his "bride," the Church. This joyous occur-

rence was of such magnitude that while he was here on earth no one was allowed to "mourn."

> "Jesus said to them: 'The sons of the bridal chamber are not able to mourn as long as the bridegroom [me] is with them ... but when he [the groom] is lifted up from them [in the Ascension], then they will [even] fast.'" Matthew 9:15

The Church on earth, as Jesus' bride, is composed of "many members" [1 Corinthians 12:12]. Thus, in Jesus' story of the groom of Matthew 25:1-13, there is not one but ten virgins seeking to be his bride. They each have a lamp, with oil as a fuel to keep the lamp burning. A problem arises however when the groom is delayed in coming that night; therefore, there is a need to have more oil to keep the lamps going longer. But only five of the ten virgins have extra oil! These virgins are accepted into the Heavenly Wedding of the groom. The others are told by the groom: 'I do not know you!' [v. 12]. Those who were <u>not accepted</u> into the wedding feast were not prepared.

Two passages come to mind in this regard. First. St. Paul's 1 Corinthians 11:29 statement that some do not recognize the Body of Christ in the consecrated bread.

> "He who eats [the consecrated Bread] and drinks [the consecrated Wine] unworthily, eats and drinks judgment to himself [by] not discerning the Lord's Body." 1 Corinthians 11:29

Second. The statement of Jesus that one must receive into oneself [like a bride] the Flesh and Blood Presence of the Lord.

> "Unless you eat the Flesh of the Son of Man and drink his Blood [take his Flesh and his Life Presence into yourself] you have no [eternal] life in you." John 6:53

Finally, there is the wedding itself in Heaven for the Lamb of God! The bride of Jesus at this wedding is the Church.

"Let us rejoice ... for the marriage of the Lamb [Jesus] has come and his woman [the Church] has prepared herself ...clothed in bright, clean linen ... her acts are holy ... fortunate are the ones called to this dinner of the marriage of the Lamb." Revelation 19:7-9

"Porter with a Wineskin"
Niko Pirosmani (c. late 18th-early 19th century)
Courtesy of Wikipedia

22.

New Wine in New Wineskins

The New Wine, of which Jesus speaks in Mark 2:22, is the Eucharist. This parable of Jesus is reported in three of the four NT Gospels.

> "No one puts new wine into old wineskins; otherwise, the [new] wine will burst the [old] wineskins, and both wine and skins will be destroyed. Rather new wine is put [only] into new wineskins." Mark 2:22 [Mt 9:17]

When Jesus speaks of New Wineskins what does he mean? A "wineskin" was a bag made of animal skin, usually of a goat, used in carrying wine. At one end of this bag was a spigot with a cork stopper from which a person could drink. In NT times there were no plastic bottles; and glassware was still primitive by modern standards. Furthermore, wine was more than a recreational drink in Jesus's time because water supplies were not chlorinated and were therefore sometimes dangerous to drink. No one knew that microscopic pathogens could cause disease until about 1850 AD. They knew, however, that something in polluted water caused disease. The alcohol in wine helped prevent this.

Jesus's use of the term "wineskin" was simply another word for "person". The term "new wineskin" referred to a person who had been baptized into the Body of Christ and was therefore ready to receive the "new Wine" of Christ in the Eucharist. The term "old wineskin," or "old man," referred to a person who had not yet been "baptized" into the Body of Christ. Such a person, when eventually baptized "into Christ," was also spoken of as a "new man," or as a "new creation."

Jesus is, therefore, saying here that "New Wine," namely himself [wine transformed by the consecration at Mass into his Blood – meaning his Life] should be put into "New Wineskins," namely into those persons who have been baptized.

"Baptism now saves you." 1 Peter 3:21

"For many of you as have been baptized into Christ have put on Christ." Galatians 3:27

"If anyone is in Christ [he or she] is a new creation." 2 Corinthians 5:17

"That he [Christ] might create in himself one new man." Ephesians 2:15

"Put away the former behavior of the old man who was corrupted by desires of deception ... and put on the new man created by God in righteousness and holiness and in truth." Ephesians 4:22 & 24

If one has been "baptized into Christ," he is a "New Wineskin." If one receives the Blood of Christ, as in the Eucharist, he receives the "New Wine." "New Wine," the Eucharist, belongs in "New Wineskins," members of the Body of Christ.

The meaning here is I am in Christ [through Baptism] and Christ is in me [through the Eucharist]. These two sacraments make possible "Communion" with the Lord. The Lord reaches down, as it were, from Heaven to speak with communicants – especially during Mass.

"And the one [Lord] sitting on the throne [in Heaven] said: 'See, I am making all things new' [New Wine for New Wineskins]." Revelation 21:5

3rd-century fresco in the Catacomb of Callixtus
Courtesy of Wikipedia

23.

Orders to Consecrate

Jesus did not leave his Church adrift upon the sea. Jesus rather selected twelve men to learn from him and then go forth as leaders into the future, after Jesus had "ascended to where he was before" [John 6:62].

In this section, four passages from Matthew's Gospel will be especially examined. They are those passages that give the Apostles, and their successor bishops, the powers of "binding and loosing" in the Name of the Lord. This is important for the consecration of the Eucharist.

First, Matthew 10:1 forward. In this passage Jesus chose twelve men to especially train. He required these men to make personal sacrifices: restrictions that touched upon their family life and personal property [Mt 10:37; Luke 18:22 & 28-29]; and also required a life-long commitment to the work [Luke 9:62].

"Jesus called to himself ... twelve Apostles ...
first Simon, the one being called Peter [mean-
ing rock]; and Andrew his brother; and James
the son of Zebedee, and John his brother;
Philip, and Bartholomew; Thomas, and Matthew the tax man; Simon the Canaanite, and
Judas Iscariot who betrayed him. These
twelve men Jesus sent out." Matthew 10:1-5

Second, Matthew 16:18-19. In this passage Jesus will
single out Simon to be the leader of the Twelve Apostles. He will give Simon a new name, that of Peter.
This name, in the Aramaic language, spoken by Jesus,
is "Rock." The amazing point here is that this name,
Rock, was only used of God in the OT, and was also
used by Paul in the NT to speak of Jesus [1 Cor 10:4].
So, Jesus is here transferring a name used of himself
to Simon.

"The spiritual rock that followed them [on the
Exodus] was the Christ." 1 Corinthians 10:4

"Jesus ... said to him [Simon]... 'I say to you:
You are [now] Peter [meaning Rock], and

upon this rock I will build my Church.'" Matthew 16:18

But Jesus will go even further in his transfer of authority; he will give Peter, and his successor popes, "the keys to the Kingdom of Heaven" [v.19]. This symbol of "the keys" goes back to the ancient world when population centers were surrounded by a sizable wall having one large opening or gate. This gate was opened and closed "by keys." The ruler or person in charge within the city had possession of the keys. This concept also applied to kingdoms. For example, the kingdom of David, Israel, also had someone in charge next to the king. In today's world we would call this person the "prime minister." There is a case demonstrating this in Isaiah 22, where the king's minister, Shebna is being replaced by Eliakim in the kingdom of Judah about 701 BC. "Thus says the Lord Yahweh of hosts. Go to the steward Shebna who is over the house [of the king] [and say]: What have you [done] here?' ... I will [therefore] drive you from your position ... I will call my servant Eliakim ... And I will cloth him with your robe and your sash ... and your [governing] authority I will give into his hand. And he shall be a father [pope?] to the dwellers of Jerusalem and to the house of Judah. And I will put the key of the house of David on his shoulder: so that he shall open, and no one shall shut; and he shall shut, and no one shall open." Isaiah 22:15 & 19-24

This was the background that Jesus drew upon in assigning Peter the authority of the keys. In the NT, Jesus himself was identified with these words from Isaiah.

> "Says the holy [one], the true, the one having the key of David [Jesus], the one opening and no one will close, and closing and no one opens." Revelation 3:7

Jesus will then assign these powers to Peter. Notice the similarity of the words from Isaiah 22:22, Revelation 3:7, and Matthew 16:19.

> "I [Jesus] will give to you [Peter] the keys of the Kingdom of Heaven, and what you bind on the earth, will have been bound in Heaven, and what you loose on the earth will have been loosed in Heaven." Matthew 16:19

The power "to bind" applies especially to the consecration of bread and wine in the Eucharist. The celebrant at a specific Mass gets his authority from the bishop who consecrated him and whom he represents. That bishop's authority has in turn come from a successor of St. Peter who passed on the authority of "binding" to that bishop.

The authority of "loosing" is the key to the sacrament of reconciliation, or the forgiveness of sins. This "loosing" power was given by Jesus to the Twelve Apostles on Easter Sunday eve.

> "He [the risen Jesus] breathed on them [the Apostles] and said: 'Receive the Holy Spirit. If you forgive the sins of any, they are forgiven them; if you retain the sins of any, they are retained [not forgiven]." John 20:23

It was Christ's way of giving every sinner assurance that his or her sins, after baptism, have been forgiven when confessed.

One final point about the Eucharist and Peter. Jesus said of himself: "I am the Good Shepherd; I know my sheep ..." [John 10:14]. Jesus would later give this authority and the care of his sheep to Peter. He said the following.

> "When they ate a meal Jesus said to Simon Peter ... feed my lambs ... shepherd my sheep ... feed my sheep." John 21:15-17

Peter is given, as a result, this responsibility of protecting and feeding the followers of Jesus. Feeding Jesus' sheep is especially related to the Eucharist. Thus, through the ages Popes have selected various priests to be bishops, giving them the necessary powers of consecration and discernment.

Third, Matthew 18:18. In this passage, Jesus gave the powers of binding and loosing to the other Apostles of the Twelve. The successors of these Twelve Apostles would eventually be the "bishops" of future ages [the NT Greek word means "overseers"]. Jesus was establishing his Church, to carry on his mission after he had returned to the Father [John 14:2].

> "Amen I [Jesus] say to you [the Twelve]: 'As much as you bind on earth will have been

bound in Heaven, and as much as you loose
on earth will have been loosed in Heaven."
Matthew 18:18

This promise of "binding" the bread and wine into the
Body and Blood of Christ is no ordinary power. And
the authority to "loose" people of their sins is no ordinary power. In fact, Christ made these powers very
personal. He promised the following.

"The one hearing you hears me, and the one
setting you aside, sets me aside ..." Luke 10:16

Fourth, Matthew 28:19-20. This passage defines how
far the powers of the Twelve were intended by God to
go. The initial group was not meant to be a transitory
part of history. These men were directed "to make
disciples of all nations," directing them toward the incarnate Lord and his Kingdom. "All nations" is a very
large slice of reality, a multi-generational undertak-
ing.

"The eleven apostles traveled into Galilee ...
Jesus spoke to them, saying: '... make disciples of all nations, baptizing them in the

Name of the Father and of the Son and of the
Holy Spirit … and behold I am with you [es-
pecially in the Eucharist] all days until the full
completion of the age.'" Matthew 28:19-20

The "Acts of the Apostles" is a history book detailing
events in the early Church. In the very first chapter of
Acts, the infant Church, the Twelve, sets out to re-
store its number after the loss of Judas. Peter, the chief
Apostle, stood up and stated that the open position
once held by Judas had to be filled. This initial apostolic group was a corporate structure that had to be
maintained.

"In those days [after Jesus' Ascension, v.9],
Peter stood up in the midst of the brothers,
and said [the number of persons present was
about 120]: 'Men and brothers … Let his [Ju-
das'] days be few, and let another take his office … let another take his authority as bishop
[his oversight] …' And they stood two up
[nominated them]: Joseph, the one called
Barabbas … and Matthias. And they prayed,
and said: 'You Lord who know the hearts of
all men, show which of these two you have

chosen, to take this service and apostleship, from which Judas fell ... And the lot fell on Matthias and he was numbered with the eleven Apostles." Acts 1:15 & 20 & 23-26

Bishops, or "overseers" [in Greek], were carefully chosen even during the first century. The bishop's two essential duties were to teach the truth about Christ and his Kingdom [liturgy of the Word] and to feed the flock [liturgy of the Eucharist]. St. Ignatius of Antioch demonstrated these two essential duties of the bishop. He speaks of the Eucharist in the seven letters he wrote on the way to Rome in 107 AD.

"Take note of those who hold unorthodox opinions ... They abstain from the Eucharist ... because they do not confess that the Eucharist is the Flesh of our Savior Jesus Christ; Flesh that suffered for our sins and which the Father in his goodness raised up again [to be our 'living Bread']. They who deny the gift of God [the Eucharist] are perishing in their disputes ... See that you follow the bishop ... Let no man do anything connected with the Church without the bishop. Let that be

deemed a proper Eucharist which is adminis-
tered either by the bishop or by one to whom
he has entrusted it [i.e., the priest]. Wherever
the bishop shall appear, there let the assembly
also be – just as wherever Jesus Christ is, there
is the Catholic Church." *Letter to the Smyrnaeans* 6-8

"Origin of the Eucharist"
Juan de Juanes (mid-late 16th century)
Courtesy of Wikipedia

24.

Real Presence

In the Eucharist, the risen Christ is Present under the appearances of consecrated Bread and Wine. As the Eucharistic Lord, Christ is received inside the communicant as the essential eternal Food. His Presence, within the one receiving, is a "real Presence." The Lord is there especially to speak with the person and to give them his special peace [John 14:27].

In a similar, but fundamentally different way, the Lord promised to be externally Present whenever two or three persons would meet together in his Name. The topic of such a meeting could be anything, as long as it involved the Lord. Also in this situation, he promised to be Present, even though unseen. This invisibility resembled in some way his sudden "disappearance" at the town of Emmaus; when after consecrating bread, and giving it to his two disciples, he became invisible [Luke 24:31]. He was invisibly Present in the consecrated Bread, so he no longer had to be present in his human body. Thus the disappearance!

"My presence shall go with you, and I will give
you rest." Exodus 33:4

"For where two or three are gathered together
in my Name, there I am [or will be] in the
middle of them." Matthew 18:20

In this kind of divine manifestation, the Lord would
be Present outside of two or three persons, rather
than inside individual persons as is true with the Eucharist. This situation is an example of the great mystery surrounding God.

"For my thoughts [as God] are not your
thoughts; neither are your ways my ways, says
the Lord." Isaiah 55:8

This invisible Presence of the Lord Jesus is mysterious!

"I heard a great voice out of Heaven, saying:
'Behold, the tabernacle of God [the Body of
Christ] is [always] with men, and he will
dwell with them, and they shall be his people."
Revelation 21:3

25.

Mass in the Book of Revelation

The Book of Revelation is saturated with the elements of "worship." There are churches, Sunday worship, altars, lampstands, candles, elders, vestments, angels, saints, white [baptism?] garments, sign of the cross, singing, penitential prayer, Gloria, alleluia, incense, golden chalices, harpists, silent contemplation, the Book of the Lamb, the sacrificial Lamb, hidden Manna, marriage of the Lamb with the Church, and the great Supper in Heaven.

It is the vision of Heaven coming down to earth within the Mass and in the judgment of evil surrounding the Church that forms the main themes of the Book of Revelation. And in the Mass it is Christ, the Lamb of God who stands at the altar, speaking through the priest, making himself personally Present in the consecrated Bread and Wine of the Eucharist.

What follows is a look at various passages from the Book of Revelation that throw light upon elements of the Mass.

<u>Sunday Mass</u>

> "I [John] was in the spirit on the Lord's Day [Sunday]." Revelation 1:10

<u>Mass Invitation</u>

> "I [Jesus] have stood at the door and I knock, if some … open the door, I will go in to him [liturgy of the Word], and I will dine with him and himself with me [liturgy of the Eucharist] … After this I looked, and there was in Heaven a door that stood open." Revelation 3:20 & 4:1

<u>Sign of the Cross</u> [to begin Mass]

> "We have marked the servants of our God with a seal on their foreheads [tracing of the cross]." Revelation 7:3

"I looked, and there was the Lamb [Jesus] standing on Mount Zion [in Jerusalem]! And with him were 144,000 who had his name and the Father's name written on their foreheads." Revelation 14:1

Confession of Sin

"Remember from where you have fallen; repent, and do the first works." Revelation 2:5

"Remember what you have … heard; keep it, and repent." Revelation 3:3

"I [Jesus] rebuke and instruct … be zealous then, and repent." Revelation 3:19

Liturgy of the Word

The Gloria

"The four living ones [angels] … are saying day and night without rest: 'Holy, holy, holy, Lord God the Almighty, who was and is and is to come … give glory and honor and thanks to the one seated on the throne, who lives forever and ever.'" Revelation 4:8-9

"They sing the song ... of the Lamb [Jesus], saying: 'Great and marvelous are your works, Lord God Almighty! Right and true are your ways, King of the nations! Lord, who will not fear and glorify your name? For you alone are holy ... all the nations will come and worship before you." Revelation 15:3-4

Church Sermons

"To the ... church in Ephesus write: 'These are the words of him who holds the seven stars in his right hand." Revelation 2:1

"To the ... church of Smyrna write 'These are the words of the first and the last [Jesus], who was dead and came to life." Revelation 2:8

"To the ... church in Pergamum write: 'These are the words of him [Jesus] who has the sharp two-edged sword." Revelation 2:12

"To the. ... church in Thyatira write: 'These are the words of the Son of God [Jesus], who has eyes like a flame of fire." Revelation 2:18

"To the ... church in Philadelphia write: 'These are the words of the Holy One [Jesus], the true one, who has the key of David." Revelation 3:7

"To the ... church in Laodicea write: 'These are the words of the Amen, the faithful and true witness [Jesus], the origin of God's creation." Revelation 3:14

Liturgy of the Eucharist

The Altar

"I saw [in Heaven] under the sacrifice place [the altar] the souls of those having been slaughtered for the Word of God and for the testimony they had given." Rev 6:9

"Another angel with a golden censer came and stood at the sacrifice place [the altar]; he was given a large amount of incense to offer

with the prayers of all the saints on the golden
altar that is before the throne. And the smoke
of the incense, with the prayers of the saints,
rose before God from the hand of the angel."
Rev 8:3-4

Elders [Priests]

"They appointed elders [priests] for them in
each church [founded on their missionary
journey], and with prayers and fasting, com-
mended them to the Lord." Acts 14:23

"Around the throne [of God in Heaven} are 24
[other] thrones and seated on these thrones
are 24 elders dressed in white robes with
golden crowns on their heads." Rev 4:4

"You [the Lamb, Jesus – v. 8] made them a
Kingdom and priests for our God [the Father]
, and they will be kings on the earth." Rev 5:10

"The seventh angel blew his trumpet, and
there were loud voices in Heaven, saying: 'The
kingdom of the world has become the King-

dom of our Lord and of his Christ, and he will be King forever and ever.' Then the 24 elders who sit on their thrones before God fell on their faces and worshiped God, saying: 'We give you thanks, Lord God Almighty.'" Rev 11:15-17

Church Music

"I heard a sound from Heaven ... the sound I heard was the sound of harpists ... and they sing a new song before the throne [of God] ... and before the elders. No one could learn that song except the 144,000 who had been brought from the earth. These are the ones not stained with women [living celibate lives], for they are virgins; these are the ones following the Lamb [Jesus] wherever he goes." Rev 14:2-4

High Priest at the Altar

"I saw seven golden lampstands, and in the middle of the lampstands I saw one like the Son of Man [Jesus], clothed with a long robe and with a golden sash across his chest [clothes of the High Priest in the Jerusalem Temple]." Rev1:12-13

"He [Jesus], because he remains forever, has a priesthood that does not pass away. ... He has no need as did the [OT] high priests, to offer sacrifice day after day ...for the sins of the people; he did that once for all when he offered himself [on the cross]." Hebrews 7:23 & 27

"Come measure the temple of God and the altar and those who worship there ... There are ... two lampstands [on the altar] that stand before the Lord of the earth." Rev 11:1 & 4

Lamb: the Eternal Sacrifice

The title "Lamb" appears twenty-eight times in the Book of Revelation. The Lamb sacrificed is eternally present. Jesus is not in time as we are; God has no time. Likewise God is not bound to any specific location in space; God is not space-bound. The Lamb of God [Jesus] is Present on many altars at any one time.

"I saw in the middle of the throne ... and in the middle of the elders [priests], a Lamb [Jesus] standing as if it had been slaughtered, having seven horns [the fullness of power] and seven eyes [the fullness of knowledge] ..."
Rev 5:6

"Twenty-four elders fell before the Lamb [in Heaven], each holding a harp and golden bowls [chalices] full of incense. that are the prayers of the saints; and they sing a new song [hymn], saying: 'Worthy are you to receive the small book ... for you [the Lamb, Jesus] was slain and with your Blood purchased for God those from every tribe and language, people and nation.'" Rev 5:8-9

"I saw and I heard the voice of many angels encircling the throne [in Heaven] ... and the elders, all of whom numbered myriads of myriads ... saying in a great voice: 'Worthy is the Lamb [Jesus], the one having been slain, to receive power and ... honor and glory and blessing." Rev 5:11-12

"In the small book of the life of the Lamb [Jesus], the one having been slain from the foundation of the world." Rev 13:8

Lamb as the Eucharist

"To everyone who conquers [3:12], I [Jesus] will give to him the hidden Manna [the Eucharist: 'I Am the living Bread' John 6:51]." Rev 2:17

"I [Jesus] stood at the door and I knock [on a person's heart] … if someone … opens the door [of himself], I will go into him and will dine with him and himself with me." Rev 3:20

"The Lamb [Jesus] at the center of the throne [in Heaven] will shepherd them [with Eucharist food] and will guide them to … the waters of [eternal] life." Rev 7:17 [John 21:16]

"I heard the sound of a great crowd … saying: 'Hallelujah! … Let us rejoice … for the marriage of the Lamb has come … Blessed are those who have been called to the supper of the marriage of the Lamb." Rev 19:6-9

"I saw an angel having stood in the sun and he shouted in a great voice, saying: ' ... Come, gather for the great supper of God.'" Rev 19:17

<u>The Lamb's bride is the Church.</u>

End of "Mass"

"Amen. Come, Lord Jesus!" Rev 22:20

This prayer at the end of the Book of Revelation is not only about Jesus's return in glory at the end time. It is also about his appearance in the Eucharist during Mass. We say "Amen" to his coming, before and during the time of Communion.

The Mass was described by St. John Paul II as "Heaven on earth," explaining in more detail that " the liturgy we celebrate here on earth is a mysterious participation in the heavenly liturgy." [Angelus Address of Nov. 3, 1996] In other words one might say that Mass is Heaven on earth, or that one goes to

Heaven during Mass. Either way, Mass is an incalcu-
lable reality!

26.

Last Supper

Some Christians teach that Christ's work was fully completed when he said on the cross: "It is finished," just before he died [John 19:30]. If this is true, then there would be no need of Christ to be a "mediator" between God the Father and the individual sinner of today.

"There is one God, and one mediator of God and men, the [divine] man Christ Jesus, who gave himself as a ransom [for sin] on behalf of all." 1 Timothy 2:5-6

"He [Jesus] is the mediator of a new covenant [announced at the Last Supper] so that those who are called may receive the promised eternal inheritance …" Hebrews 9:15

"He [Jesus] holds his priesthood permanently, because he continues [in it] forever. Thus, he is able for all time to save all those

who come to God [the Father] <u>through him</u>;
always living to make <u>an appeal</u> on behalf of
them." Hebrews 7:24-25

"Christ Jesus ... having been raised [from the
dead], who's at the right [hand] of God [the
Father], making <u>appeals on behalf of us</u> [Paul
included?]." Romans 8:34

"We [believers!] have an advocate with [God]
the Father, Jesus Christ the righteous ." 1 John
2:1-2

There would also be no need for the Eucharist or the
Mass even though Christ's "do this in remembrance
of Me" was given as a command at the Last Supper
[Luke 22:19 & 1 Corinthians 11:24-25]. If Christ's
work was truly "finished," all one would need to do to
be "saved" and eventually go to Heaven would be to
accept Christ's work by "faith alone." However, if
"faith alone" was the sole pathway to Heaven, why is
the NT filled with warnings about proper behavior
for believers? These warnings tell believers that they
will not go to Heaven if they do not persevere in good

works, "faith working through love" [Gal 5:6], or what one might call a "holy" lifestyle. The following behavior texts are from just one book in the NT, the Book of Hebrews 3:1-2...3:6...3:12-14...4:1...4:11 ...4:13...6:4-6...10:26-27...10:36...12:4...12:14... 12:16-17...12:25... etc.

There are at least three reasons why the phrase: "It is finished" does not mean the end of Jesus' work, nor an easy life of faith for his followers.

First. Jesus' work was "finished," "from the foundation of the world."

> "The life of the one [Lamb, Jesus] slain from the foundation of the world." Revelation 13:8

> "The works [of Jesus] were finished from the foundation of the world." Hebrews 4:3

> "You were redeemed ... before the foundation of the world, but revealed now in these last times for you ..." 1 Peter 1:19-20

One must keep in mind that the divine Jesus is not bound in either space or in time. In God, there is no time.

Second, Scripture says that Jesus' work will not be finished until his "Second Coming" at the end of the world.

> "He [Jesus] holds his priesthood permanently, because he continues [in it] forever."
> Hebrews 7:24

> "We have a great high priest who has passed through the heavens, Jesus, the Son of God."
> Hebrews 4:14

> "Every high priest [such as Jesus] … is appointed to serve God [the Father], offering both gifts and sacrifices on behalf of sins." Hebrews 5:1

> "But if some[one] might sin [after Baptism] we have an advocate with [God] the Father,

> Jesus Christ the righteous. He is the reconciling sacrifice for our sins." 1 John 2:1

Some would say, of this, that if a person "accepts Jesus as their personal Lord and savior" they will be forever saved; meaning that they will possess "eternal security." This is what is usually meant by accepting Jesus' "finished work on the cross." However, this does not end the matter of sin! Hebrews 10:26-27 discusses this point. It says that Jesus' "sacrifice on the cross" no longer applies if a believer continues to sin without trying to improve.

> "If we [Christians] willingly sin, after receiving the knowledge of the truth, there will no longer remain the sacrifice [of Christ] for sins; but [rather] the waiting for judgment and fire [an aloneness outside of Heaven]." Hebrews 10:26-27

Third. The words, "It is finished," more appropriately refer to the Last Supper and to the consumption of the last cup of wine of the Passover Meal – on the cross! The Last Supper was a Passover Meal. In this scripted meal, four cups of wine, and only four cups, were consumed. The first cup was served before the meal began. The second cup was served when the main course of lamb was served. The third cup, the "cup of blessing," was served at the end of the main course. It was at this point in the meal that Jesus "consecrated" bread and wine to create his own "Body and Blood" Presence. Then, after giving the Twelve Apostles this new-Presence of himself in "Communion," he left the Last Supper with his Apostles, but without drinking the fourth cup of wine, the "cup of consummation." He and the Apostles went rather to the Garden of Gethsemane where Jesus prayed. Jesus prayed: "Father … remove this cup from me …"; the cup of his impending death [Mt 26:39]. In other words, he prayed that the Father would remove the fourth cup of the Passover Meal, the "cup of consummation." Hours later, at the cross, Jesus refused to drink a cup of wine that was offered him before he was crucified. Only when Jesus was near death, on the cross, did he agree to drink what turned out to be the fourth cup of the Passover Meal. And then he uttered the words: "It [the Passover Meal] is finished!"

Pope Benedict XVI celebrates the Eucharist at the canonization of Frei Galvão in São Paulo, Brazil on 11 May 2007. Courtesy of Wikipedia.

27.

Memorial Sacrifice

At the Last Supper, Jesus consecrated ordinary bread and wine to be his Body and Blood Person. After doing this action, he said to his Apostles: "Do this [likewise] in remembrance of me!" [Luke 22:19 & 1 Corinthians 11:24]

These words of Jesus in the NT are recorded in the Greek language. The Greek word used here for "remembrance," by both Luke and Paul, is "anamnesis." While there were several other Greek words that could have been used to mean "remembrance," Luke and Paul chose "anamnesis." They chose this word, because it was the only Greek word meaning "remembrance," that was specifically connected to the topic of "sacrifice."

In other words, the remembrance or memorial spoken of by Jesus, was associated with sacrifice. The Eucharist was not a mere pious remembering of the Last Supper, or a friendly "fellowship meal" as some would have it. This latter idea was rejected by Paul, when he said to the Corinthians: "When you meet together [for fellowship] it is not the Lord's Supper [the Eucharist] that you eat." [1 Corinthians 11:20]

When Jesus said: "Do this in remembrance of me," one has to examine the previous sentence to see what the word "this" meant. That sentence reads as follows: "This is my body which is given [in sacrifice] for you." [Luke 22:19] One can therefore see that, the phrase "Do this," associated with the word "anamnesis," refers to the giving of the body of Jesus in sacrifice.

In the OT Book of Leviticus 24:7-9 the word "anamnesis" is used in a passage concerning "bread sacrifice." In this passage various Eucharist-like words are used: bread memorial, continual sacrifice, priests, incense, covenant, and eating.

> "You shall put on each row [of the Breads of the Presence] pure <u>frankincense</u>, and it shall be <u>bread for a memorial [anamnesis]</u>, a fire <u>offering</u> to Yahweh. On every Sabbath day he [the priest Aaron] shall arrange it before

Yahweh <u>continually</u>, being from the people of Israel, a <u>never-ending covenant</u>. And … Aaron and his sons [the priests] <u>shall eat it</u> [later] in the holy place…" Leviticus 24:7-9

This passage involving a "bread sacrifice" resembles the Eucharist in several ways: it is offered under the appearance of bread, is a perpetual sacrifice, is offered on every Sabbath, is eaten by priests in a holy place [or church], and involves an eternal covenant. Jesus' words at the Last Supper, therefore echo the words and structure of this bread-sacrifice in the OT Book of Leviticus.

28.

Sacrifice within Mass

Christ died once on the cross at Calvary. However, since Christ does not repeatedly die, some have argued that "the Mass" itself cannot be a sacrifice. This argument is prefaced by the false idea that all OT sacrifices involved the shedding of blood and death. This is not true. Many sacrifices in the OT did not involve the killing of animals. Two such examples from the OT are "cereal offerings" and the offerings of "prayer and fasting." One particular example of "prayer and fasting" is that of Moses before God to remove the sin of his people for assembling the Golden Calf.

"I [Moses] fell down before Yahweh ... for forty days and nights; I ate no bread and drank no water; because of all your sins [idol worship] ... I was afraid of the anger and fury that Yahweh had against you ... I also prayed for Aaron [my brother] at that time." Deuteronomy 9:18-20

In the NT, there are also examples of bloodless sacrifice. For example, in Romans 12:1, Paul tells his people to "present your bodies as a living sacrifice, holy and well-pleasing to God, your reasonable service ..." And in 1 Peter 2:5 Christians are told that they are living stones being built up into a spiritual house ... with a holy priesthood to bring up [into Heaven] spiritual sacrifices well-accepted by God [the Father] through Christ."

The Eucharist itself is a non-bloody, living sacrifice. The Mass represents the event of Calvary involving the divine Person, Jesus, who is not bound in space or by time. At Mass the priest takes the place of Christ, and like Christ, separates both consecrations. First, he consecrates the bread to become Jesus' sacrificial Body. Then he consecrates the wine to become Jesus' sacrificial Blood. This separation of Blood from Body represents the "timeless death of Jesus" upon the cross. However, Jesus' "Flesh and Blood" Presence upon the altar, also speaks simultaneously of his resurrection – neither event being bound in time. God has no time!

Mass is offered around the world at varying times, often in many locations at one specific time. These situations explain why there are "sacrifices," in the plural, when speaking of the Mass offering.

> "Heavenly better sacrifices than these [OT examples]." Hebrews 9:23

In other words, there is no contradiction between the one and the many sacrifices. One, however, must keep in mind the fact that the divine Son is not bound in either space or in time. He can be in many places at one time. The Mass, therefore, is a great mystery hidden in God's very Being!

"The Disputation of the Holy Sacrament"
Raphael (1509-1510)
Courtesy of Wikipedia

29.

Transubstantiation

The Church uses the word "transubstantiation" to describe the change of bread and wine into the Body and Blood of Christ. This term was adopted by the Fourth Lateran Council of the Church in 1215 AD. Previous to this date other terms were used to describe this miraculous action which was prescribed by Christ when he said: "Do this," at the Last Supper. Some of the earlier terms used for this momentous change were transfigured, transformed, and converted.

Transubstantiation uses two concepts to differentiate the change. The first concept is that of "substance," meaning the underlying reality of a thing [its essence]. The second concept is that of "accidents," meaning qualities such as color, size, smell, taste, and texture. A simple example of these two concepts might be that of two lemons, one green and the other yellow. The "substance" of the two lemons is the fact that both of them are lemons. The "accidents" in this case would be the green or yellow color, and perhaps the smaller size of the unripe green lemon.

Transubstantiation fundamentally requires a person to believe in God's creative power. If one believes, for example, that God created the universe out of nothing, then it becomes easy for him or her to believe that God can change one thing into something else; the example here being bread and wine into his own Body and Blood Presence.

There are examples in the NT of transubstantiation-like miracles previous to Jesus' action at the Last Supper. One example of such a miracle occurred at the wedding feast at Cana in Galilee. In this week-long event, the groom ran out of wine for his guests [John 2:1-11]. Jesus' mother, Mary, alerted Jesus to this problem. In solving it, Jesus had several large stone jars filled with water. When the head waiter tasted the 120 gallons of water, it had instantaneously been changed into a fine grade of wine. This was an introduction to Jesus' later work at the Last Supper, where he changed red(?) wine into his own Blood.

A second transubstantiation-like miracle that occurred before the Last Supper was that of the Feeding of the 5000 [Matt 14:19 & Mk 6:41 & Luke 9:16 & John 6:11].

In this miracle, Jesus changed five loaves of bread into enough bread to feed many thousands of people. Later, at the Last Supper, he would change one loaf of bread into his own Body, and then share parts of it, being fully himself in each part, with his Apostles.

There are also transubstantiation-like occurrences in nature that one can examine. For example, the "substance" of water is water. However, this water can exist in three "accidental" forms: as ice below 32 degrees F., as ordinary water at room temperature, and finally as an invisible vapor above 212 degrees F.

God in his infinite sensitivity has allowed the "accidents" of bread and wine to remain visible in the transubstantiation process. However, to believe that Christ is Present in the Eucharist, requires true "faith." Faith is one of the fundamental virtues. To be "saved," one is required to have the humility of faith.

Faith in the Eucharist is an essential component of faith, a required ingredient within the "life of faith."

> "All who eat and drink without discerning the Body [of Christ], eat and drink judgment to themselves." 1 Corinthians 11:29 [John 6:53]

"Christ with the Eucharist: 'This is my body.'"
Juan de Juanes (c. 3rd quarter of the 16th century)
Courtesy of Wikipedia

30.

This is My Body - the Gender Lock

Some modern Christians react in the same way that certain Jews reacted when Jesus described the "New Manna" of the NT era. Jesus said the following:

> "The bread that I will give is <u>my flesh</u> … for the [eternal, Heavenly] life of the world." John 6:51

Certain Jews reacted to this statement in the following way.

> "The Jews … said: 'How can this man give us <u>his flesh</u> to eat?'" John 6:52

Some people of our own time also reject these words of Jesus. They further reject his words at the Last Supper when he said: "This [bread] is my Body…" Luke 22:19

"Take [the bread], eat, this is my Body." Matt 26:26

Disbelievers of the present time confidently claim that Jesus did not really mean that the bread he was holding in his hand at the Last Supper had become his Body. They rather say that the word "This," in Jesus' statement: "This is my Body," refers only to the bread - but not to his Body. And they further state that, since the bread continues to look like bread, it can only be a representation of the body of Jesus. In other words, they are saying it cannot literally be the Body of Jesus, meaning that the bread is only a symbol.

But certain other people, who have looked into these matters, have some questions of their own to ask. First. They ask how it can be that Jesus, who said that he was "the truth" [John 14:6], could have lied about this issue of his Presence. They continue on, saying that Jesus' statement was very clear. Jesus said: "This [bread] IS my Body." If he had meant for the bread to be a mere representation of his body, he could have used very different words. For example, he could have said:

"This [bread] represents my body."

or "This [bread] symbolizes my body."

or "This [bread] will stand for my body."

or even simpler ...

"This [bread] will mean my body."

However, Jesus wanted to be crystal clear; he wanted to eliminate all speculation.

He said simply: "This [bread] IS my Body."

These words of Jesus have come down to us in the Greek language of the NT. In the Greek language, nouns are put together with adjectives in a special way. In the Greek language adjectives are either male, female, or neutral in gender. Furthermore, the gender of an adjective used has to match the gender of the noun it describes. For example, a masculine adjective goes only with a masculine noun. A feminine adjective goes only with a feminine noun. And a neuter adjective goes only with a neuter noun.

Jesus used the following words that are recorded in Luke 22:19.

"This [bread] IS my Body which is given for
you."

In the above sentence the word "This" is a neutral adjective.; and the word "bread" is a male noun. This
means that the neutral adjective, "This," does not refer to the male noun, "bread" – because their <u>genders
do not match</u>. Rather, the neutral adjective, "This," refers to the neutral noun, "body." The reason "This" refers to "body," is that their <u>genders match</u>. The word,
"This," therefore refers only to the "Body" of Christ –
not to the starter bread. In other words, "This" bread
has become the "Body" of Christ. Those trying to
change the meaning of Jesus' words cannot therefore
succeed.

The "This," after the consecration, is Jesus' "Body."
Those who say that "This" refers to the bread are
wrong.

In like fashion, in Matthew 26:28, Jesus' words concerning his blood are as follows.

"Drink you all of it; for this [wine] IS my
Blood of the new covenant ..."

In this quotation the word, "this" is a neutral adjective that refers only to the neutral noun, "Blood." The neutral adjective "this" cannot correspond to the male noun "wine."

In other words, in the statement of Jesus, "This" has become his "Blood" – by the power of his words. "This" cannot refer to the wine as some would say.

One final point. The words or intentions of Jesus are powerful, even when used by others, such as priests with "orders" at Mass. An example of the power of Jesus' can be seen in Acts, where St. Peter cured a paralyzed man by using the power of Jesus.

> "Then Peter said: ' … In the name of Jesus Christ of Nazareth rise up and walk!' … And he [the paralyzed man] leaped up and walked and entered with them into the Temple, walking and leaping and praising God." Acts 3:6-8

At Mass, the priest carries out the order of Jesus, to "Do this" as Jesus had done it at the Last Supper, giving us his Body and Blood Self in "Holy Communion."

31.

Paul's Eucharist

"Paul the Apostle"
Valentin de Boulogne (circa 1618-1620)
Courtesy of Wikipedia

St. Paul reported on the actions and words of Jesus at the Last Supper in 1 Corinthians 11:23-26 and then went on to offer some thoughts of his own [v. 26-30]. It is these thoughts of Paul that this chapter will report and comment upon.

"I [Paul] received from the Lord [Jesus] that which I delivered to you. That the Lord on the same night he was betrayed took bread; and when he had given thanks, he broke it, and said: 'Take, eat: This is my Body ... Do this [action] in remembrance of me.' ...He also took the cup [of wine] ...saying: 'This cup is the new covenant in my Blood: you do this [action] ... in remembrance of me.'" 1 Corinthians 11:23-25

This statement of Paul was written in 53 AD, about twenty years after the resurrection of Jesus. This section will examine the next four verses in Paul's thought.

First, Paul's initial comment addresses the mystery of the Mass. He says that the Mass presents both the death and the resurrection of Jesus. The reality is that God is not bound in space, as we are, or in time. In fact, God has no time. Therefore, Jesus is the timeless sacrifice at every Mass. In addition to this, his resurrection is manifest at the moment of Communion, when those attending Mass receive his Eucharistic Presence.

"As often as you eat this Bread and drink the cup [of Wine] [the Eucharist] you proclaim the death of the Lord [Jesus] until he comes [again]." 1 Corinthians 11:26

The usage in 1 Corinthians 11:26 shows that the Eucharist was intended to proclaim the death of Jesus, as well as his resurrection. What Jesus announced at the Last Supper has little to do with the "fellowship meal" of some modern Christians. Paul says as much in verses 20-22.

"When you come together ... it is not to eat the Lord's supper ... everyone takes his own supper ... do you not have houses to eat and drink in? Do you despise the Church of God...? I praise you not!" 1 Corinthians 11:20-22

Second, Paul addresses the issue of not believing in the real presence of Jesus in the Eucharist. He says that such a person receives Communion "unworthily."

> "Whoever eats the Bread or drinks the cup [of Wine] of the Lord unworthily will be guilty of [profaning] the Body and Blood of the Lord. But let a man prove [or examine] himself, and only then let him eat the Bread and drink from the cup [of Wine] [the Eucharist]." 1 Corinthians 11:27-28

Notice the word "unworthily." Why would a person, eating and drinking common food, ordinary bread and wine, be doing so in an unworthy manner? The point is that the "Bread and Cup of the Lord" is not common food. It is the Body and Blood Presence of the Lord. The Eucharist is not a mere symbol!

Paul then goes on to say that those who eat unworthily are "guilty" of profaning the reality of the Lord's Presence in the Eucharist. The word "guilty" is usually associated with a crime. For example, the Pharisees accused Jesus of blasphemy and then said: "He is guilty of death!" [Matthew 26:66]. Again, if the Eucharist were merely a "symbol," no one would be "guilty" of abusing it. No one could be said to be guilty of wrong-doing unless the bread had in fact become Christ's Body and Blood Presence!

Third, Paul says that if one does not believe that the "consecrated" bread is the Body of Christ, "judgment" will come upon oneself. In the NT, the term "judgment," usually refers to "condemnation."

> "All who eat and drink without discerning the Body [of the Lord], eat and drink judgment [meaning damnation] upon themselves." 1 Corinthians 11:29

But again, if the Eucharist was only a "symbol," judgment or condemnation would not make sense. It would be unintelligible. That is why Paul speaks of the problem of "not discerning the Body" of the Lord.

Fourth, Paul says in verse 30 that this lack of acknowledgement of Jesus' identity in the Eucharist and reverence for his Person was also causing physical problems among the people of Corinth in Greece. He says that their insufficient Eucharistic belief and reverence were causing many to be bodily weak and sick, and some to have even died. In other words, their spiritual deficiencies were spilling over into their physical lives. Their not discerning the Lord's physical Body as Present, under the appearance of

Bread and Wine, was bringing God's early "judgment" upon themselves. The Eucharist was not to be treated as common food.

Lastly, in this same 1 Corinthians letter, Paul also compared the Corinthian Church to the people of the Exodus. God had given the people of the Exodus great miracles to help them. God had baptized them in the Reed Sea and had also given them the miraculous bread-like Manna for food on their journey to Canaan [modern Israel]. "Our fathers ... all went through the sea ... [and] were baptized into Moses... and all ate the same spiritual food [the Manna] ..." 1 Corinthians 10:1-3

Then Paul tells the Corinthians that God has given them an even greater miracle. He says that the "spiritual food" of the Exodus was ordinary bread, but now God has given them the Eucharist, himself, as their food for the journey to Heaven. Paul says in effect that the Eucharist is no ordinary common food. He makes this especially clear in 1 Corinthians 10:16-17.

> "The Cup of blessing that we [with orders]
> bless, is it not a sharing in the Blood of Christ?
> The Bread that we break, is it not a sharing in
> the Body of Christ? Because there is one
> Bread, we who are many are one Body, for we
> all partake of the one Bread." 1 Corinthians
> 10:16-17

Here Paul says that the Corinthian Christians are all one Body in Christ because they all receive the same one [consecrated] Bread. How could such a thing be if the bread consumed by them was merely common bread? Paul's point is that the "blessing that we bless" has changed common bread into the Eucharist, into the Lord's very Presence. And it is through the power of his Person that we are all one – the Body of Christ, the universal Church [Ephesians 1:22-23]

32.

Spirit in the Eucharist

A year before the Last Supper, Jesus gave what has come to be called the "Bread of Life Discourse." It is located in John 6:22-71. There is the introduction [verses 22-34], the discourse proper [v.35-59], and various reactions to it [v. 60-71]. The discourse proper is an introduction to the Eucharist, which is the fulfillment of the OT Manna.

In this discourse, between verses 51-56, Jesus told his followers six times, that he is going to give them a new food to eat that will give them eternal life [v.54]. This food will be his own Flesh and Blood [verses 53-56]. He does not tell them that it will be provided under the appearances of Bread and Wine. He will do that a year later, at the Last Supper [Luke 22:19-20]. The Jews present at the time, were shocked, because Jews in general did not eat the blood of any animal – much less that of a human being.

> "Be sure not to eat the blood, for the blood is
> the life [within the animal], and you shall not
> eat the life with the flesh." Deuteronomy 12:23

Here in John 6, Jesus uses the term "flesh" [sarx in Greek] rather than the term "body" [soma in Greek], which he would later use at the Last Supper when speaking of his Eucharistic Body. However, in both places, Jesus uses the word "blood" [heima in Greek]. St. Paul himself used both words, sarx and soma, to mean "body" in various of his letters.

> "If you live by the flesh [sarx], you will die; but
> if you put to death the practices of the body
> [soma] you will live." Romans 8:13

Jesus described the Eucharist as his own "Flesh;" four times between verses 51-56 in John 6. Then, after some rejection of his usage [see v.60], Jesus made the following statement.

> "The spirit [or soul] is the one making us live,
> the flesh benefits nothing; the words which I
> [Jesus] have spoken to you are spirit and life."
> John 6:63

What did Jesus mean by this statement? Some have taken the words, "the flesh benefits nothing," and have applied them to verses 51-56 where Jesus speaks of the Eucharist. They argue that Jesus is retracting what he said in verses 51-56 about "his flesh". They say that Jesus has given us eternal life by coming into the world in the flesh; but that now the "flesh benefits nothing."

However, Jesus is not talking about "his own flesh" in v. 63; he is not taking back what he said about his flesh in verses 51-56. Rather, Jesus is talking here about the problem of "flesh verses the spirit" in everyone's life. He is saying that our spirit gives us life, while our flesh wars against it [see Romans 7:14-25].

> "With the mind I myself [Paul] serve the law of God; but with the flesh the law of sin." Romans 7:25

St. Paul, in his writings, speaks about how the spiritual man can discern spiritual truths because he is led by the Holy Spirit. The Spirit especially witnesses to the truth of the Eucharist.

"We speak not in man-like wisdom, but in words taught by the [Holy] Spirit, spiritual things judging spiritual things." 1 Corinthians 2:12-13

"The Comforter, the Holy Spirit, whom the Father will send in my Name; he will teach you all and will remind you of all that I [Jesus] said to you." John 14:26

Paul means here that "the flesh" interferes with a man discerning spiritual truths. That is why "the flesh benefits nothing" [v.63]. Furthermore, because "the Spirit" helps one to understand spiritual truths, the "Spirit is the one making us live" [v. 63].

That is also what Jesus meant when he spoke to Nicodemus.

"The one born from the flash [of human parents] is flesh, and the one born from the Spirit [of God] is spirit." John 3:6

The Spirit, like the wind, can intervene anywhere, in any one's life, at any time. However, to insure a person of the Spirit's Presence, Peter advised being baptized.

> "Peter, said to them: 'Repent [change your mind], and be baptized each of you on the name of Jesus Christ so that your sins will be forgiven; and you will [for sure] receive the gift of the Holy Spirit.'" Acts 2:38

33.

Eucharist in the Early Church

Most of the NT documents were written between the years 30-70 AD. However, the 27 documents of the NT were not formally gathered into one "NT book" until the Council of Carthage in 397 AD. Until that time the documents were kept in various churches and read especially during Mass. They were, however, widely known among the growing Christian populations. This is evidenced among the early Church fathers, the learned generations following the passing of the Twelve Apostles. The Church fathers quote these NT scriptures thousands of times. One can almost construct a copy of the NT from the NT quotations recorded in the writings of the early Church fathers.

These writings from the first three centuries cover many important topics. This chapter will focus on only one topic of their work: the Eucharist.

Didache c. 35 AD

The Didache [Greek for "Teaching"] may be one of the oldest Christian documents outside of the NT. It is thought by some scholars to date to about 35 AD.

> "In regard to the Eucharist, you shall give thanks thus. First, in regard to the cup: We give you thanks Father, for the holy vine of David … made known to us through Jesus your Son … In regard to the broken bread: We give you thanks, our Father, for the life and knowledge which you have made known to us through Jesus your Son … Let no one eat or drink of the Eucharist with you except those who have been baptized in the name of the Lord…" Chapter 9:1

> "On the Lord's Day [Sunday] …gather together, break bread and give thanks [the Eucharist], after confessing your sin so that your sacrifice may be pure. Let no one who has a quarrel with his neighbor join you until he be reconciled, less your sacrifice be defiled. For this is that which was proclaimed by the Lord:

'In every place and time let there be offered to me a pure sacrifice [Malachi 1:11]" Chapter 14:1

St. Clement of Rome, Pope c. 68 AD

There are several lists of the early popes that exist. Clement is fourth on the lists of Hegesippus and Irenaeus in the second century: Peter, Linus, Anencletus [Cletus], and then Clement. Some scholars believe that Clement wrote his letter to the Corinthian Church about 68 AD. There are two reasons for this: First, Clement speaks of the animal sacrifices happening in the Jerusalem Temple. This Temple and the city of Jerusalem were destroyed in 70 AD. After that date the Jewish faith no longer offered animals in sacrifice to God. Second, the deaths of Peter and Paul are referred to as recent events within his letter. It is thought that both apostles died during Emperor Nero's persecution of Christians between 64-68 AD.

"Continual sacrifices are offered ... but only in Jerusalem, and even there ... only in front of the inner Temple on the altar of sacrifice; and the [animal] offering is first inspected for blemishes by the high priest and the ministers." Chapter 41:1-2

"Consider the noble examples of our own generation. Through jealousy and envy the ... pillars were persecuted and persevered even unto death. ... Peter who suffered through unwarranted jealousy ... went to the place of glory ... Through jealousy and strife Paul showed the way ... of endurance. Seven times he was in chains ... giving his testimony before rulers he was [also] taken from this world." Chapter 5:1-7

"Do we not have one God [the Father], one Christ, and one Spirit of Grace poured out upon us? And is there not one calling [to leadership] in Christ? ... Love unites us to God. Love covers a multitude of sins. Love endures all things, is long-suffering in everything. There is nothing vulgar in love, nothing haughty. Love makes no schism [divisions]; love does not quarrel; love does everything in unity ... For the sake of the love which he had for us did Jesus Christ our Lord, by the will of

God [the Father], give his Blood for us, his Flesh for our flesh [the Eucharist], and his life for our lives [on the cross, covering our sins]." Chapter 46:6 & 49:5-6

St. Ignatius of Antioch 50? -107 AD

Ignatius was the bishop of Antioch in Syria. Antioch was a large city in the first century. The Roman Emperor, Trajan, had Ignatius arrested and brought to Rome where he died in the Colosseum. En route, the saint wrote seven letters to various church communities. Ignatius may have been born about 50 AD, before St. Paul went to Corinth to speak with its people about Jesus.

"Give ear to the bishop and to the presbyters [priests] with an undivided mind, breaking one bread [the Eucharist - Acts 2:42], which is the medicine of immortality, the antidote against death, enabling us to live forever in Jesus Christ." *Letter to the Ephesians* 20:2

"I [Ignatius] have no taste for corruptible [ordinary] food, nor for the pleasures of this life.

I desire the Bread of God [the Eucharist], which is the Flesh of Jesus Christ [John 6:51], who is the seed of David [Mark 12:35]." *Letter to the Romans* 7:3

"Take care, then, to use one Eucharist, so that whatever you do, you do according to God. For there is one Flesh of our Lord Jesus Christ [consecrated Bread], and one cup in the union of his Blood [consecrated Wine]; one altar, as there is one bishop with the presbyters [priests] and my fellow servants, the deacons." *Letter to the Philadelphians* 3:4

"I make the Gospel my refuge [liturgy of the Word], as if it were the flesh of Jesus [liturgy of the Eucharist] … The [OT] prophets we also love, because they too have announced the Gospel; they hoped in him [Jesus] and awaited for him." *Letter to the Philadelphians* 5:1-2

"They [outsiders] abstain from the Eucharist and from [related] prayer, because they do not confess that the Eucharist [consecrated

Bread] is the Flesh of our Savior Jesus Christ; Flesh which suffered for our sins and which [God] the Father, in his goodness, raised up again. They who deny the gift of God [John 4:10] are perishing in their disputes [1 Corinthians 11:29]." *Letter to the Smyrnaeans* 7:1

"Let no one do anything of concern to the Church without the bishop. Let that be considered a valid Eucharist which is celebrated by the bishop, or by one whom he appoints [the priests]. Wherever the bishop appears, let the people be there; just as wherever Jesus Christ is, there is the Catholic [universal] Church." *Letter to the Smyrnaeans* 8:1-2

St. Justin Martyr 148-155 AD

Justin was born about 100 and died a martyr in 165 AD. He was a student of philosophy, who spent much of his life explaining Christianity to the ruling party in Rome. His "First Apology" was addressed to the Roman Emperor and contains an outline of the Catholic Mass - much as we find it today.

"We call this food [of the Mass] Eucharist; and no one is permitted to partake of it, except one who believes our teaching … and has been washed [baptized] … for the remission of sins and for regeneration, and is thereby living as Christ intended. For not as common bread nor common drink do we receive these; but since Jesus Christ our Savior was made incarnate by the word of God and had both flesh and blood for our salvation, so too … the food which has been made into the Eucharist by the Eucharistic prayer set down by him [at the Last Supper] … is both the Flesh [consecrated Bread] and the Blood [consecrated Wine] of the incarnated Jesus." *First Apology* 66

"On Sunday, all those who live in cities or who dwell in the countryside gather in a common meeting [Sunday Mass]. And as long as there is time the Memoirs of the Apostles ['Memoirs which they produced … called Gospels' – 66] or the writings of the [OT] prophets are read. Then, when the reader has finished, the president [bishop or designate] verbally gives a warning and appeal for the imitation of these good examples [the Sunday sermon]. After this, we all rise together and offer prayers [the offertory], and ... when our prayer is ended, [common] bread is brought forward along with [common] wine ... Then the president gives thanks to the best of his ability, and the people [eventually] call out their assent, saying 'Amen.' Then there is the distribution to each participant [at Mass] of the Eucharistic elements [consecrated Bread, the Body of Christ and consecrated Wine, the Blood of Christ]; which are sent out [later] with the deacons to those who are absent [perhaps sick]. Those who are wealthy then ... contribute whatever they care to give , and this collection is placed with the president, who aids orphans and widows and those who through sickness or any other cause are in need." *First Apology* 67

St Irenaeus of Lyons 180 AD

Irenaeus [140-202 AD] was born in Smyrna [Izmir in modern Turkey]. He was a student of St. Polycarp

[69-156 AD], the bishop of Smyrna. Polycarp had, as a young man, been a "hearer" of the Apostle John. Irenaeus at 37, became the bishop of Lyons [in modern France], in the year 177 AD. Beginning about 180, he wrote his large work, entitled, "Against Heresies."

Irenaeus taught that Christ established the Eucharist as the new sacrifice of a new covenant. In this new covenant, or "new testament," Christ himself is the sacrifice and the one making that offering. The priest stands in for Christ at Mass. This sacrifice of the Mass is the fulfillment of all the sacrifices of the OT people. Irenaeus spoke of Malachi's prophesy of a "pure offering" for all peoples [Malachi 1:11 & 14]. In the Eucharist, Christ offers himself under the appearances of the bread and wine, which have now become his Body [consecrated Bread] and his Blood [consecrated Wine] of the NT era.

> "He [Jesus] took from among creation that which is bread, and gave thanks, saying: 'This is my Body.' The cup [of wine] likewise, which is also from the creation of which we belong, and declared it to be his Blood.

He taught the new sacrifice of the new covenant, of which Malachi, one of the [OT] prophets, had signified beforehand: 'You [Jewish priests] do not do my will … and I will not accept a sacrifice at your hands. For from the rising of the sun to its setting my Name is to be glorified among the gentiles, and in every place [upon earth] incense will be offered to my Name, and a pure sacrifice'… By these words he [God] made it plain that the former [OT] people will cease to make offerings to God; but that in every place sacrifice will be offered to him, and indeed, a pure one [consecrated Bread and Wine] for his Name is to be glorified among the gentiles [all non-Jewish peoples]." *Against Heresies* 4, 17, 5

"The bread over which thanks [the consecration] has been given is the Body of the Lord, and the cup [of consecrated Wine] his Blood … For as the bread from the earth, receiving the invocation of God, is no longer common bread but the Eucharist consisting of two elements, earthly and heavenly; so also our bodies, when they receive the Eucharist, are no

longer corruptible but have the hope of resurrection into eternity." *Against Heresies* 4, 18,
4-5

<u>Tertullian</u> c. 200 AD

Tertullian [160-220] was a lawyer of considerable
reputation in Rome. His Christian writings were
widely read in the Roman world.

"We should understand 'give us this day our
daily bread' [in the Lord's Prayer of Mathew
6:11] in a spiritual sense. For Christ is our
Bread [the Eucharist], because Christ is [our
eternal] Life, and bread is life. He said, 'I Am,
the Bread of Life;' and shortly before that: '
Bread is the Word of the Living God which
comes down from Heaven.' [John 6:31-35]
And then, so that his Body be included in the
term bread [he said]: 'This is my Body' [the
Eucharist]. In asking, therefore, for our daily
bread, we petition for continued existence 'in
Christ' and indivisibility from his Body."
Prayer 6, 2

"Having taken bread and having distributed it to his disciples, he [Jesus] made it his own Body, saying: 'This [Bread] is my Body.'" Against Marcion 4, 40

St. Clement of Alexandria 202 AD

Born in Athens, Clement [150 – 215 AD] became the director of the school of catechumens in Alexandria about 200 AD.

"To drink the Blood of Jesus [as consecrated Wine] is to share in his immortality ... the drink [of Wine] plus the Word [of God] is called the Eucharist ... Those who partake of it in faith are sanctified in body and in soul." *The Teacher* 2, 2

"Hear the Savior: ' ... I am he that feeds you. I give myself as Bread [the Eucharist], of which he that has tasted experiences death no more; and I supply daily the Drink of immortality [the consecrated Wine]. I am the Teacher of lessons concerning the highest Heaven. On behalf of you I contended with death; I [Jesus] paid the death which you owed for your former sins and for your unbelief towards God." *Who is the Rich Man that is Saved* 23, 2

Origen of Alexandria 244 AD

Origen [185-253] was the first student of NT scripture to write a manual of theology. It has been titled: "The Fundamental Doctrines."

Much of it has been lost.

> "You are accustomed to take part in the divine mysteries [of the Mass], so you know how, when you have received the Body of the Lord [the Eucharist], you reverently exercise every care less a particle of it fall [to the floor], and less anything of the consecrated Gift perish. You account yourselves guilty, and rightly do you so believe, if any of it be lost through negligence. But if you observe such caution in keeping his Body, and properly so, how is it that you think neglecting the Word of God a

lesser offence than neglecting his Body." *On Exodus* 13, 3

"He who considers that: 'Christ, our paschal lamb has been sacrificed' [1 Corinthians 5:7] knows that it is his duty to keep the feast by eating the Flesh of the Word [the Eucharist], and so he never ceases to keep the paschal feast ... he is ever striving in his thoughts, words, and deeds, to pass over from the things of this life to God. He is hastening toward the city of God." *Against Celsus* 8, 22

St. Cyprian of Carthage 251 AD

Cyprian was born about 206 AD in Carthage. His parents were wealthy pagans. Cyprian became a Christian about 246, a priest in 247, and the bishop of Carthage in 249.

In 250, the Decian persecution broke out and Cyprian had to take refuge in the hills outside the city, where he directed his people by letters to the clergy. Cyprian was martyred in 258.

"We ask and say: 'Give us this day our daily
bread.' [Matt 6:11]. ... And we ask that this
bread be given us daily, so that we who are in
Christ and daily receive the Eucharist as the
food of salvation, may not, by falling into
some grievous sin and then by abstaining
from communicating, be withheld from the
heavenly Bread, and be separated from
Christ's Body. ... He himself warns us, saying:
'Unless you eat the flesh of the Son of Man
[the consecrated Bread] and drink his blood
[the consecrated Wine], you shall have no life
in you.' [John 6:53] Therefore do we ask that
our Bread, which is Christ be given to us daily,
so that we who abide and live in Christ may
not withdraw from his sanctification and
from his Body." *The Lord's Prayer* 18

St. Athanasius c. 340 AD

Athanasius [295-373 AD] was born near Alexandria.
He was ordained a deacon in 319 and served as
bishop Alexander's secretary at the Council of Nicaea
in 325 AD. He was the principal opponent of the Ar-
ian heresy at Nicaea and supporter of the Nicene

doctrine. In 328, he was consecrated the bishop of Alexandria. During his work as bishop he was exiled five times by his enemies.

"The Savior, since he was changing OT types for the spiritual, promised them they should no longer eat the flesh of a [Passover] lamb, but his own [self], saying: 'Take, eat and drink; this is my Body and my Blood.' When we are thus nourished by these things, we also … shall truly keep the feast of the Passover." *Easter Letter* 4, 4

"You shall see the priests bringing loaves and a cup of wine, and placing them on the table. So long as the prayers of supplication and entreaties have not been made, there is only bread and wine. But after the great and wonderful prayers have been completed [the consecration], then the bread has become the Body, and the wine the Blood, of our Lord Jesus Christ." *Sermon to the Newly Baptized*

St. Ambrose of Milan 390 AD

Ambrose [333-397] was trained as a lawyer, and later, about the year 370 was given the high office of Consul in Milan. When Bishop Auxentius of Milan died, many in the city wanted Ambrose as his replacement. However, at the time Ambrose was merely studying the Christian faith. No matter! He was baptized on December 1, and one week later on December 7, 374, he was consecrated the new bishop of Milan. St. Augustine would be one of his converts!

> "Perhaps you will say: 'I see something else; how is it that you assert that I receive the Body of Christ [in the Eucharist]?' Let us prove that this is not what nature made ... For that sacrament which you receive is made what it is by the word of Christ. But if the word of Elijah [in the OT] had such power as to bring down fire from heaven, shall not the word of Christ have power to change the nature of the elements [in the bread]?" On the Mysteries 9, 50-52

St. Gregory of Nyssa 383 AD

Gregory [335-394] was the brother of Basil of Caesarea. In 371 he was consecrated the bishop of Nyssa.

> "We believe that the bread consecrated by the word of God has been made over into the Body of God the Word … it has been consecrated by the lodging therein of the Word, who pitched his tent [with us] in the flesh."
> The Great Catechism 37:9-13

St. John Chrysostom 403 AD

John [344-407] was a native of Antioch, in Syria. He met the bishop of Antioch when he was 18 and began his journey. He became a hermit, living in a cave for four years. In 381 he was ordained a deacon and a priest in 386. He then preached in the main church of Antioch from 386-397, and after that was consecrated the bishop of Constantinople.

> "Since the sacrifice [of the Mass] is offered everywhere are there then a multiplicity of Christs? By no means! Christ is one every-

where. He is complete here, complete there, one Body. And just as he is one Body and not many , though offered everywhere, so too is there one Sacrifice." Sermon on Hebrews 17, 3

St. Augustine of Hippo 392 AD

Augustine [354-430] was born in Tagaste, in north Africa. His father was a civic official and his mother was St. Monica. In 371, at age 17, Augustine went to Carthage for advanced study. In 372, his son, Adeodatus was born of his girlfriend. In 383, he became a speech and writing teacher in Milan. In Milan he met St. Ambrose and was baptized by him in 387 with his mother and son being present. His mother died shortly thereafter. He then returned to north Africa with his son who also died about 389. Augustine then studied for the priesthood and was ordained by bishop Valerius of Hippo in 391. Shortly before Valerius died in 395, he consecrated Augustine to be the bishop of Hippo. Augustine is especially known today for two books: his Confessions and The City of God.

"He [Christ] was carried in his own hands [at the Last Supper]. But, brethren, how is it possible for a man to do this? Who can understand it? … A man can be carried in the hands of another; but no one can be carried in his own hands. …Christ was carried in his own hands when, referring to his own Body, he said: 'This [Bread] is my Body.' For he carried that Body in his hands." Psalms 33, 1, 10

About the Author

Roger Skrenes, author of The Jesus Code: In the Beginning was the Word (En Route Books and Media, 2016), studied science as an undergraduate and history as a graduate.

He holds a master's degree in religion and has taught high school in Los Angeles, California, for over thirty years, including six summers in the California Youth Authority (a prison for teenage boys in Whittier, CA).

He is the father of three adult children, Mary, Mark and Therese.

www.ingramcontent.com/pod-product-compliance
Lightning Source LLC
Chambersburg PA
CBHW060043100426
42742CB00014B/2681